T0338528

The Pocket Mentor for Video Game Testing

Want to work as a games tester in the video games industry? Then this is the book for you. This book provides all the essential information and guidance you need to understand the industry and get your foot in the door.

This book covers everything, from the education you'll need, how to look for and apply for job opportunities, and the studio interview process itself. It also includes advice for what to do once you're in the role, with chapters covering how to write a bug report and creating test plans, as well as interviews with top tips from experts in the industry.

This book will be of great interest for all beginner and aspiring games QA testers looking to build their career.

Harún Ali has more than 4 years' worth of game testing experience, working on titles such as Lego Dimensions and Space MMO Star Citizen. Before working in the industry, he worked in the education sector as a game development tutor. That experience ignited a passion for educating people by volunteering as a STEM ambassador to speak at local schools, Limit Break Mentorship, and WASD, Yorkshire Games Festival, Develop:Brighton and EGX to advocate for QA and underrepresented groups within the games industry.

The Pocket Mentors for Games Careers Series

The Pocket Mentors for Games Careers series provides the essential information and guidance needed to get and keep a job in the modern games industry. They explain in simple, clear language exactly what a beginner needs to know about education requirements, finding job opportunities, applying for roles, and acing studio interviews. Readers will learn how to navigate studio hierarchies, transfer roles and companies, work overseas, and develop their skills.

The Pocket Mentor for Video Game Writers
Anna Megill

The Pocket Mentor for Video Game Testing
Harún H. Ali

For more information about this series, please visit: www.routledge.com/European-Animation/book-series/PMGC

The Pocket Mentor for Video Game Testing

Harún H. Ali

CRC Press
Taylor & Francis Group
Boca Raton London New York

CRC Press is an imprint of the
Taylor & Francis Group, an **informa** business

Designed cover image: Shutterstock

First edition published 2024
by CRC Press
2385 Executive Center Drive, Suite 320, Boca Raton, FL 33431

and by CRC Press
4 Park Square, Milton Park, Abingdon, Oxon, OX14 4RN

CRC Press is an imprint of Taylor & Francis Group, LLC

© 2024 Harún H. Ali

Library of Congress Cataloging-in-Publication Data
Names: Ali, Harún H., author.
Title: The pocket mentor for video game testing / Harún H. Ali.
Description: First edition. | Boca Raton, FL : CRC Press, 2024. |
Series: The pocket mentors for games careers series
Identifiers: LCCN 2023027271 (print) | LCCN 2023027272 (ebook) |
ISBN 9781032323985 (hardback) | ISBN 9781032323978 (paperback) |
ISBN 9781003314806 (ebook)
Subjects: LCSH: Video games–Testing. |
Video games industry–Vocational guidance.
Classification: LCC GV1469.3 .A38 2024 (print) |
LCC GV1469.3 (ebook) | DDC 794.8–dc23/eng/20230712
LC record available at https://lccn.loc.gov/2023027271
LC ebook record available at https://lccn.loc.gov/2023027272

ISBN: 9781032323985 (hbk)
ISBN: 9781032323978 (pbk)
ISBN: 9781003314806 (ebk)

DOI: 10.1201/9781003314806

Typeset in Times New Roman
by Newgen Publishing UK

Contents

Acknowledgements

Many aspects of this book come from my knowledge and life experience as a games student, teacher, and industry professional. So, while I have numerous insights into the ever-changing games industry, I thought it was important to research and learn from different people to help expand my learning, get helpful advice, and fill in any gaps in my knowledge to ensure that what I am writing about is relevant as possible to you, the reader. So, I would like to list the amazing people who agreed to be interviewed for research purposes of the book. Some of which I have quoted in this book to help give you other insights from industry professionals. Your insights have been invaluable, and I am forever grateful for your time:

- **Jaffer Shah** – Embedded Network Tester at Cloud Imperium Games
- **Andrea Nicolazzo** – Compliance Tester at Rockstar Games
- **Lukas Genever** – Talent Acquisition Manager at Cloud Imperium Games
- **Janel Jolly** – QA Development Director at EA
- **Darren Eggerton** – QA Manager at XR Games
- **Naveen Yadav** – QA Manager at nDreams
- **Jack Mamais** – Professor of Game Design at SCAD
- **Amanda Lange** – Alexa Developer Community Manager
- **Dan Gronner** – Lead QA Tester at Roll7
- **Ollie Balaam** – Senior Quality Software Engineer at Improbable
- **Tarja Porkka-Kontturi** – Director of Communications at the Global Game Jam
- **Rosie Taylor** – Communications Officer and Community Manager at Safe in Our World
- **Sky Tunley-Stainton** – Partnerships and Training Officer at Safe in Our World

Introduction

The video game industry is the biggest entertainment industry in the world and certainly one of the most unique. When you read a book, watch a film, or watch a TV show, the viewer is passive during the whole experience. The viewer has no influence on the event on the pages or screen (with notable exceptions being choose your own adventure-style books or interactive films like Black Mirror's Bandersnatch). Progression on a movie won't be halted if you don't complete a quick time event fast enough; a book won't lock you out of a chapter if you don't complete a quiz on its core themes. (There's an old Dara O Briain stand-up bit that this metaphor is borrowing from that I highly recommend watching.)

Games allow users to actively participate in a world the developers have created. You are the hero of the story; you can shape it however you want. What makes it unique is that everyone will have their own way of taking on a challenge which can make for some fun water cooler moments with your friends, you might boast about a fantastic combo you did on a boss or how you epically failed a mission by rolling the wrong way and falling off a cliff.

Gaming is so entrenched in our world that it's not a small niche; gaming is for everyone. Regardless of age or background, we have all played video games, whether at an arcade in a theme park, playing consoles in the living room, or even playing a game on our phones during a long commute. More and more people want to become a part of this ever-growing industry (and if you are reading this that means you want to as well). The games industry has a diverse range of jobs and departments you can be a part of, from art, VFX, programming, marketing, legal, to HR. No matter what department you work for in a games company, you are a part of the game industry; you are a game developer. All these different jobs and departments help breathe life into a game and help it find an audience. And quality assurance is a significant and essential part of that development process.

WHO AM I?

If it wasn't clear from the front cover, my name is Harún, and it's nice to meet you. I have loved video games ever since I was 4 years old. I grew up playing games on my uncle's old Commodore Amiga that he gave me. I then moved on to the SEGA systems like most people in Europe in the 1990s with the Master System, Mega Drive, and then eventually moved into the third dimension with the PS1 I got on my fifth birthday in 1998. Since then, I've grown up with consoles; I've seen the industry develop and evolve from the fifth generation to the current generation, which is currently the ninth generation of systems (PS5 and Xbox series X).

After finishing secondary school in 2010, I knew I wanted to study and learn more about the game development process, but I had no idea where to begin. It was only when me and my dad asked around about what software is used to make games did we learn about 3DS Max, Cinema4D, and C++. We also learnt about a game development course that I could attend at my local college.

I studied games development at Bradford College for 2 years, then went on to do Games Art at Bradford University for 3 years (yeah, I pretty much stayed as a local boy). In mid-2015, I was 21 and got my first chance to work in the games industry as a QA tester for TT Fusion (a subsidiary of TT Games). It was only a 6-month contract, but while there, I spent most of my time working on Lego Dimensions, a toys-to-life game, and a little bit of time on Lego Marvel Avengers. Unfortunately, as with many fixed-term QA testers, my contract was not renewed, so I was out of a job. I kept trying to find more QA work, but there weren't many available at the time. But then, my old FE College tutor messaged me in late 2015 to let me know there was a job at Wakefield College as a games development tutor. I ended up working there part-time and picked up some teaching hours at Bradford College. During this time, I grew to enjoy teaching; not only was I able to assist many aspiring developers, but it also motivated me to expand my knowledge of game industry software and events and keep up with current trends.

As much as I was keeping up to date with changes in the industry and expanding my network, I still felt like an outsider looking in. So I left teaching in July 2019 and returned to the industry as a QA tester for Cloud Imperium Games, the studio behind Sci-Fi MMO Star Citizen and its single-player game Squadron 42. By the end of that year, I was promoted from QA tester to environment art tester and started my new role in 2020. I stayed embedded until early April 2023, then left to work as an associate producer at No Brakes Games, known for Human Fall Flat.

WHO'S THIS BOOK FOR?

So, you might be wondering why I'm writing this book. The simple answer is that I love the games industry, not just playing games but understanding the development process, the pipelines, the intricacies of its design, and even discussing any relevant topics brewing within the industry. That love and passion for the games drove me to become a teacher. I wanted to pass on my knowledge and experiences to students and help them overcome the pitfalls and issues I faced when I was in their shoes. So, now I am hoping to pass some of my knowledge on to you, the reader.

If you already work in QA, then you may already know most of the content in this book, so it might be worth looking for a more in-depth technical testing book. This book is for someone who has just finished education or is looking for a new career path. First, I will cover the different types of jobs in QA and what skills you should develop. Then, we will explore alternative ways to build your experience, understand the recruitment process, QA interviews, and go over some of the day-to-day testing you are expected to do when you finally get that QA role. So, let's get started!

What Is QA 1

Quality assurance (QA) is any game's first and last line of defence. (Throughout this book you will see me use the abbreviation or phrases such as, QA tester or tester, these all refer to game testing. Will also see the term QA throughout this book as well which refers to both the department and the discipline of quality assurance.) QA's function is to systematically review and test a product to ensure it meets a certain level of quality, whether internal standards or meeting requirements from platform holders (e.g. Sony or Nintendo). QA will catch issues, report them, and, depending on the severity of the problems, can help production make alterations to schedules and even releases. Without an effective QA department that liaises with its members and the wider company, it can have ramifications on the quality of the final product. Other departments will be entirely focused on their work and won't have the resources to effectively do in-depth testing to see how their submissions interact with the game. This is where QA comes in, as they can meticulously test different scenarios to try and find ways to break or even exploit the game by thinking outside the box. Going beyond what the initial intentions were for a game mechanic or mission path to push the boundaries of a game to expose a fault, QA will have a deep understanding of how to play the game and will provide detailed reports with any necessary data for the developers, so they can reproduce the issues and begin working on a potential fix.

1.1 THE STIGMATISATION OF QA

QA has had many stereotypes and stigmatisation over the years from both within the industry and gamers. For example, when a game is released in

DOI: 10.1201/9781003314806-1

a buggy fashion and when it gets a negative response, sometimes you will hear people complain, "did anyone test this", "QA not doing their jobs", or the worst one is when heads of companies essentially throw QA under the bus by saying something like "our testing did not show a big part of the issues".

Relationships between QA and other developers at some companies have in the past been strained, and some may view them more like outsiders. Because of this, some departments won't view QA as part of the development team and keep them at arm's length. Some factors contributing to this could be that the QA department in some larger studios may have a dedicated studio in different cities or even countries, so QA is physically separated from the rest of the teams. Some companies may outsource most of their QA work to another company. Another reason could be that the QA team could be made up of mostly contracted workers, so a working relationship isn't fully formed due to the rotating door of new testers.

Yeah, I know the stuff I have written earlier is a bit of a downer, but now is where I flip it to a more hopeful message (yay!). The view of QA has improved a lot over the years; this can be due to QA being more embedded into the development teams and having more seats at the table during meetings. People who work alongside QA daily, like producers, know the value of QA and their determination for their work. Developers are building strong working relationships with their QA departments. They get to know them well, so any time someone has a hot take on Twitter about QA, many industry professionals from different departments and companies will defend their QA co-workers.

The general gaming public does have a better understanding and appreciation for the hard work testers put on a game, partly due to outspoken developers and news articles about working conditions, which helps give QA more exposure and humanise the department. However, there are still gaps in people's knowledge regarding the game production pipeline. I would like to see more of QA's work highlighted in behind-the-scenes footage and have more of a voice at public gaming events to showcase the diversity of roles within the industry.

A great example of this is the behind-the-scenes video on Resident Evil Village called "Making of Resident Evil Village – The Internal Struggle". The QA manager, Shutaro Kobayashi, talks about how QA provided the support and feedback to help shape gameplay towards the final product as earlier development builds were more action focused. The video also discusses how QA was brought into meetings to give their input, which helped refocus the gameplay on the horror elements. Videos like these should be more commonplace as they show how QA can provide input into a game and are part of the development process, not a separate entity.

1.2 CAN YOU MAKE A CAREER OUT OF QA?

People often refer to QA as a way of getting your foot in the door. Some will encourage people to go through the QA process to get to their dream job, whether in programming, design, or art. And while yes, it can help you progress into different departments, QA should not be seen as just a steppingstone but as a legitimate career path. Don't get me wrong; I get wanting to branch out and try out different things beyond QA. I mean, the Education and Mentoring chapter of this book will most likely be relevant to those searching for ways to grow beyond the tester role.

I spoke to a few people who work in different roles in QA about QA as a career, and I thought it would be good to highlight their comments here so you are not just getting my voice on this matter.

> *Yeah, I really love QA work; I love the investigation part of it. It feels like detective work sometimes, hunting down particularly unusual bugs, things that just don't seem to instantly make logical sense and trying to piece together bits and pieces of knowledge. I feel like if you can enjoy doing QA in that way, then it's absolutely something that you can stick with and advance through.*
>
> *Quote from Darren Eggerton*

> *Yes, you absolutely can. QA is very deep and wide; there are loads of different directions you can specialise in. Some examples include performance, security, continuous integration and delivery. For every discipline of game dev, it's useful to have a quality advocate in there. It's very deep and you can really pursue what you, what you are interested in.*
>
> *Quote from Ollie Balaam*

> *yes, it is possible because me and countless others have done it. It is becoming more and more easier to get in as the gaming industry is expanding, the need for QA is expanding. I would say it's a lot easier to get in now; it just depends on where you look and where you live as well.*
>
> *Quote from Naveen Yadav*

Can you make a career out of QA? The short answer is yes, the long answer is yes, as there are many different roles in a QA department, from technical roles such as a QA engineer or working your way up the hierarchy to leadership roles like a managerial position. But you will learn more about those later in this chapter. There is also a caveat with this question: some employers can offer full-time permanent employment, while others offer fixed-term contracts. This is not exclusive to just QA; many sectors in and outside games use short-term contracts.

1.3 HIERARCHY

Let's start by looking at the hierarchy of a QA department. In Figure 1.1, we can see a rudimentary breakdown of the organisational structure found within the QA department. Smaller companies may have a structure like this.

But a QA department can be a bit more complex than the example given in Figure 1.1. Depending on the size of the company and the complexity of its titles, you could have a department that has many specialisms and roles similar to that seen in Figure 1.2.

You can see that multiple layers work together to create an effective department. It's also worth noting that not every company will have the same order or roles, so don't take Figure 1.2 as the definitive outline of a QA department but rather as an example of what one can be. Depending on the department size, there can be multiple leadership and senior roles. For example, there can be various QA tester teams in a department, each with its own QA leads

FIGURE 1.1 Basic QA department hierarchy.

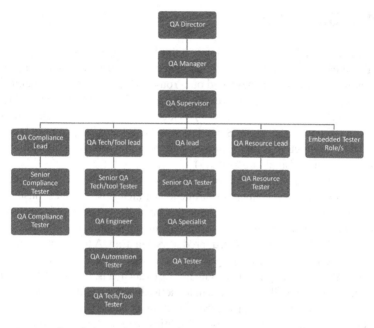

FIGURE 1.2   Detailed QA department hierarchy.

and seniors. Many big AAA companies or outsource QA will be working on multiple titles at a time, so dedicated teams will work on game X or game Y. If you are looking to move up in the hierarchy, there could be multiple job opportunities for different leadership roles. Now that we have provided a breakdown of the QA hierarchy, let's go ahead and break down the various job positions within the QA department.

1.4 THE MANY ROLES OF QA

So, you like to play games, it's your passion! You love spending hours playing the latest Open World RPG or that brand-new fighting game you downloaded from your preferred digital store. You may want to take that passion and turn it into a career. However, there is one thing to note: there is a world of difference between playing games and making them. The same can be said for testing as well. You will learn in later chapters some of the tasks a QA tester has to do to ensure all the issues in a game are found. But for now, let us look at the available roles and their responsibilities.

1.4.1 QA Testers

This is pretty much your starting point; at this level, you will be actively testing the game every day, and your role is to execute the test cases and plans that the senior and lead testers have laid out. You aren't there to play the game for fun; as a tester, you are directly responsible for finding, reproducing, and providing detailed reports with necessary evidence (videos, screenshots, etc.) on any issues found in the game. Some tasks you will be participating in include regression, destructive testing, smokes, and even playtesting (a breakdown of these tasks can be found in Chapter 9).

QA Leadership will provide you with the daily tasks; these can be based on the needs of other development departments via their producers. For instance , when a new location or level comes into the game, the testers may be requested to focus on this new content for an estimated amount of time. If a new mechanic has been recently added or updated, producers can ask QA to test these and see how they work within pre-existing levels. As a tester, you won't have to worry too much about creating and organising test cases and plans; you need to focus on filling these in. You will pass tests with no noticeable defects and provide details of any test cases with issues that are still passable or issues that fail a test case.

QA testers can have extra responsibilities such as creating and updating email flare threads that highlight any major critical or blocker issues to leadership around the company. Flaring issues are vital as they allow producers to assign these to the correct person to fix, which will need immediate attention. You may also provide regular updates to the senior and lead tester about the progress of current test assignments (e.g. test suites). You may also be required to do a handover comment, messages, or emails to the QA team about what has been worked on today. These messages can list the bugs seen and even what outstanding tests are left to be completed. Graphs can also accompany these updates to provide a visual representation of the state of the overall game, certain levels, or even features.

1.4.2 Compliance Tester

Suppose a company is working on a game that is being published digitally, physically, or both on consoles. In that case, the developers need to ensure that they meet the requirements of the platform holders such as Sony, Microsoft, and Nintendo. If a game does not comply with the guidelines and regulations of the platform holders, then a game could be prevented from being released until the issues that failed the compliance guidelines are resolved. That isn't to say games that fail these tests won't get released on their intended dates. Some companies can request waiver forms from the platform holders to allow submissions to go through (these can go through but with caveats). Developers will have fixes for these issues in patches, but as a tester that isn't something for you to worry about, as those types of decisions are made by leadership. A compliance tester focuses on testing how the game interacts with the console hardware, peripherals, and systems to ensure that it meets the platform holders' regulations. The types of testing will be the same as usual QA, such as regression, smoke tests, and test plans, but the tests and bugs will be based on the platform holder's compliance guidelines. I spoke with Andrea Nicolazzo, a compliance tester for Rockstar Games, to learn more about the role and discussed some of the differences between regular QA testing and compliance.

> *For example, save data, we try to mess around the save data as much as possible; I don't think QA does that. They mostly deal with the content of the game. We try to stress the console, the menu of the console, rather than the game itself; that's the main difference.*
>
> *Quote from Andrea Nicolazzo*

Save data isn't the only example; you will have to check if the achievement/ trophy systems are working as intended and test for any exploits. Some tests you may not usually consider are how the game interacts with console menus, such as suspending software and using menus while the game is suspended. Ensure any console hardware features are functioning correctly with the game; for example, the Nintendo Switch has detachable controllers, motion controls, and different controller methods unique to that system. All these will need thorough testing to ensure they meet compliance guidelines.

Being familiar with the guidelines of the platform holders is vital to your work, as you will be referring to the documentation quite frequently. Also, these documents get updated, so you must keep your knowledge as up to date as possible. Compliance testers can learn the different standards of major platform holders but can specialise in one system.

> *Some of us were trained in multiple platforms, so we could switch roles sometimes, but there are teams dedicated to specific consoles.*
>
> *Quote from Andrea Nicolazzo*

The guidelines are written in a way that they can be broadly used across any game. As a compliance tester, you will need to interpret the text to see how it fits different titles, as Andrea explains:

> *You need to interpret the guidelines 'cause the guidelines, of course, are always written in a generic way because they need to apply to every game. Whatever game you have in front of you, it might not always match, but you still need to be able to find a way to see how it applies to that.*
>
> *Quote from Andrea Nicolazzo*

1.4.3 Localisation Tester

Games are released to a worldwide market; as such, they can't just cater to one language. This big blue ball we call Earth has thousands of spoken/written languages; now, no game can provide text and audio for all of these. Most games will support various European languages and some East Asian languages. A few may also have South American languages, and many games have Arabic language options. Companies will have people translate all text in the game into different languages. The translated text will then be incorporated into the game in subtitles, interfaces, heads-up displays (HUDs), etc.

The job of localisation QA is to test the game with a focus on the text of the language you are assigned. It's crucial to be fluent in the language you are checking, as you must ensure the grammar and punctuation within the game are correct. Andrea Nicolazzo, who spoke about his role in compliance, also discussed with me his previous role as a localisation tester:

> *know your language, how it works, all the grammar rules, all the expressions. It's a like a proof-reader job but a little bit different.*
>
> *Quote from Andrea Nicolazzo*

It's essential to think about the context of words or sentences; some words can be translated in different ways, which can completely change the meaning of a phrase or sentence, which may confuse or mislead players. Even slang terms or idioms could make no sense when they have literal translations, if that's the case, then a localisation tester could point this out and suggest alternative text. How the text appears in games is also a vital piece of testing, you need to ensure no overlapping, culling, or formatting issues. For example, some words can be longer than their English counterparts, creating problems for UI or dialogue boxes with limited space.

Most localisation testing jobs do not require any official qualification in specific languages, but you do need to showcase excellent linguistic knowledge in said language. To prove this to a potential employer, you may be required to do a test during the hiring process to demonstrate a comprehensive understanding of a particular language.

1.4.4 QA Tech Roles (Tools Tester, Engineer)

When people think about QA testing in games, they will think it's primarily black box testing. This might be true of some companies, but for others, more technical QA testing roles can be available, which employ white box testing (see Chapter 9 for more information on black box and white box testing). This section will be more of a general overview of the roles and responsibilities you can expect from technical QA roles.

With QA tech roles, you will be focused on testing the game engine and other software development tools. Many companies can have their own in-house game engine, for example, Ubisoft's Snow Drop engine and id Software's id Tech engine, to name a few. Even companies that use third-party engines like Unity and Unreal may customise and create in-house tools to work with the engine. Even new features and updates to engine tools or the engine itself will need testing; this is where tech roles such as QA tools tester can come in. These roles require more technical knowledge as you need some understanding of game engines. In addition, you will need to build test cases around testing these tools.

Some roles, like QA engineers, will also utilise other technical aspects such as understanding scripting/coding languages for instance Python, Java, C#, or C++. As a QA engineer, you may be expected to create, execute, and manage automated testing processes. Debugging is another aspect of the engineer role; you may find yourself using software such as Visual Studio to read call stacks, scripts, and other lines of code to find any issues, help maintain its quality, and help towards better optimisation. Ollie Balaam works as a senior quality software engineer and discussed with me his experiences in a technical QA role:

> *Scripting is an interesting one. So if you work as QA, even if you don't consider yourself particularly technically skilled, or you don't come from a computer science background or anything like that, you are going to have to run scripts because you work with engineers.*
>
> *Because you are working with technical people, they will explain things to you and be patient with you, but they will expect you, to some*

> *extent, meet them halfway. So you won't always get "Here we printed out on a disc for you to test in your home console". You'll get sent builds that you need to run weird hacky commands on to make work.*
>
> *Quote from Ollie Balaam*

Multiplayer games also have testers that look over the back-end services to look for any errors; they also use headless clients. This automated testing system simulates a large number of people loading into the front end or a server to help see how it holds up under that kind of pressure. Ollie explains the differences between game testers and technical testers.

> *The quality games engineers in the clients, they are testing from the perspective of the gamer. I am in the developer environments, testing from the perspective of a developer. So, I spend a lot of my time in video game editors, such as Unity and Unreal, in Visual Studio, looking at code. There's also lots of other pieces of infrastructure that go into building a game.*
>
> *For instance, continuous integration, build machines and pipelines is a really large part of my job. Version control systems, such as GIT and Perforce, looking at logs and metrics. I focus almost exclusively on online multiplayer games, so a lot of my work is Finding network errors or opportunities for network optimization.*
>
> *Quote from Ollie Balaam*

1.4.5 Embedded QA Tester

This was a role I was unaware of until working at Cloud Imperium. Embedded testers have been assigned to a particular department as their go-to person for testing needs. You act as a go-between for your assigned department and the rest of QA. You will specialise and learn the intricacy of your assigned departments' pipeline. Departments such as art, design, AI, and characters can have an embedded tester assigned to them. Jaffer Shah has worked at Cloud Imperium as an embedded tester for several years, and he explains the role as such:

> *You are more in contact with the developers themselves. You work closely with them, you get to experience what they go through. You also get to test features before it filters out to general QA. So you act more like a messenger between general QA and the developers. You specialise in that area, and people go to you for any issues. Or if your developers have any issues, they come to you, and then you can liaise with the other departments to get any information that they don't know about.*
>
> *Quote from Jaffer Shah*

Embedded QA can be a mix of general testing in the game as well as more technical testing as you may find yourself using the game engine more frequently for a sanity pass, regressing issues, testing existing or upcoming in-house tools that help aid in the development process, as well as other third-party-associated software that is used by the department you are assigned to.

Applying for an embedded tester position with a background in a particular subject will be an advantage. Take my pervious role as an embedded environment art tester for instance; it required me to have some understanding of the art pipeline and process. Due to my educational background and teaching experience, I knew well about 3D software and material pipelines such as physically based rendering. This helped me get the role, and already having a fundamental knowledge of games art allowed me to learn the company's workflow and tools more efficiently.

The benefit of working as embedded tester is that you are working directly with the developers, providing updates to them, and talking with them about issues and testing. This makes for an ideal position to transition into a department role naturally. You will already be in a prime position to do so, as you will understand the work process and tools used. You can start by taking on extra responsibilities such as bug fixing or assisting with tasks just so long as you have discussed this with your lead or line manager beforehand.

Most of the time, embedded roles are not externally advertised. These are usually advertised internally, so if you already work as a QA tester, your managers may inform the department about internal openings like embedded positions. If there is a position in your field of interest, apply for it; even if you're just a couple of months into your main QA testing role, there is no harm in applying. I was hesitant to apply for the embedded environment art job because I was barely 3 months into my role, I felt that maybe I was too new to apply, but many of my peers encouraged me, which helped me find the confidence to go for it.

Now not all game companies utilise embedded testers. Some companies may have a studio dedicated purely to QA or have not put the structures in place to provide embedded testing. In my opinion, embedded testing is a massive benefit to the QA department and other departments as it can give synergy between QA and active development.

1.4.6 Senior QA Tester

A senior tester is an expert tester who has excellent knowledge of the QA process. Dan Gronner gives an excellent description of what it means to be a senior:

> *Being an exemplary QA tester, being able to work with other people at different levels, cooperating, coordinating effectively with your line manager, your peers and anyone who reports to you.*
>
> *Quote from Dan Gronner*

At this level, you will be taking on more responsibility, you will have a hand in writing test plans, and you can be a point of contact for other testers, producers, and developers. Seniors can help lead a team of testers on whatever tasks have been scheduled by the lead testers. Even with the added responsibility, seniors are still actively testing the game, making them your first point of contact. Because the QA lead has duties outside of the day-to-day testing, such as being a part of production meetings and other administrative duties, seniors will work closely with the QA lead to keep them well informed about what's happening. This is so they are up to date on the progress of a task and the team.

> *Eyes and ears on the ground in the game and in amongst the team on behalf of the lead, while the leads will have responsibility outside of QA.*
>
> *Quote from Dan Gronner*

Some seniors may also have the responsibility of training new testers. This could be mentoring them one-to-one to ensure that new testers are up to the department standards. Some seniors can also create test cases for game mechanics, set up test plans, and ensure these tests are as up to date as possible, as the game can go through different iterations. For instance, level flows can be altered or dropped, and even the game mechanics can change.

1.4.7 Lead QA

This role is usually for someone very seasoned and will be given multiple responsibilities on a project, including leading a team of testers. A lead will schedule and maintain the day-to-day testing to ensure that work is being completed efficiently and that the quality of work is high. Efficiency is key, as leads need to make sure that they prioritise tasks according to the needs of the production schedule, different departments, and even the company. Leads are usually the ones that create and maintain test cases and plans. This responsibility can be shared between seniors and leads, with the lead taking more ownership of them.

Due to the responsibilities and tasks of being a lead, they won't spend as much time in the game to test it as a senior or QA tester. Leads will have various administrative tasks, such as working alongside management to develop policies and procedures. They can also train new staff, do performance reviews for QA testers, and be involved with the recruitment process.

Leads will provide managers with relevant data, comprehensive updates, and reports on the state of the game or sections of the game. This data can also be used during production meetings, which leads will also be a part of as they act as a point of contact within the QA department and for other departments. They will have a close working relationship with production, providing them with any support needed and continuously communicating back and forth any updates from the production side, development teams, and QA department.

1.4.8 QA Manager

Managers oversee the whole department. Multiple managers can work for a specific company due to workload, such as numerous projects or many in-house testers to supervise. Another reason can be if a company has multiple studios, each one could have its own QA department, which will need oversight.

Managers typically don't test the game daily like the other QA testers, that's not to say they won't play builds or participate in playtesting every so often, but their primary responsibility is the planning and organisation of the QA process for the studio's projects. Naveen Yadav and Darren Eggerton are both QA managers, and both discussed their roles and responsibilities with me.

> *QA managers don't typically test. I can test if I want or need to. I can jump on a multiplayer session with the team if they need an extra hand. Or if I've got a single-player game, I can also just give it a quick check on how it's doing.*
>
> *Quote from Naveen Yadav*

Many responsibilities come with running a department. Managers will oversee the budget that has been allocated to QA. This budget can be used for recruiting, hardware, or other resources. You may also allocate total hours for testing the game or specific aspects of the game as that data will be used in the production project schedule.

> *But more often than not, most of my work will be through emails or spreadsheets. A lot of it is resource and budget planning. If we have an internal budget, we want to keep within that budget. So we need to hire X amount of people around a certain date and make sure we're not going over budget.*
>
> *Quote from Naveen Yadav*

They will have a holistic overview of the state of the project. With this knowledge, they will present reports to production, studio leadership, and stakeholders. Said reports can contain a list of serious issues to inform leadership about and to provide QA's verdict about levels or locations within a game (I mentioned this a little in the Leads earlier). This can help give leadership realistic expectations on the final product, which would help production and development make any necessary changes to the schedule, update existing features, and then prioritise specific bugs brought up during these meetings.

Managers are in constant communication with various departments to help ensure they feel supported or even highlight any issues preventing the QA team from doing their work. As a manager, you must advocate for QA's needs and support your team members.

> *Making sure that my team have work to do, making sure that they're not getting blocked by things and making sure that they're happy and feel fulfilled and are unimpeded, just able to do their best work.*
>
> *Quote from Darren Eggerton*

Having constant communication with other departments allows managers to understand what is currently in development, the state of a feature or level, and deadlines to determine when QA can begin the testing procedures (creating test cases, scheduling time for testing, etc.).

Usually, we talk directly with production and the development team, like programming, art, see what's coming up. Depending on deadlines, like if we're coming up to some kind of VRC submission (Virtual Reality Check) or, an FQA submission (framework of quality assurance), we'll start focusing on TRCs (Technical Requirements Checklist) long before then, that kind of thing. It's mostly just scheduling and finding out what the upcoming tasks are.

Quote from Darren Eggerton

They can also be points of contact for external partners, such as any outsourcing QA companies that the department is utilising, and even communicating with representatives of platform holders like Sony, Microsoft, and Nintendo regarding compliance.

Talking to a lot of external stakeholders. So, whoever you're publishing with or developing with, you'll need to talk with them. If you're working with Sony, for example, you'll have a point of contact at Sony who you would have a lot of communication with.

Quote from Naveen Yadav

1.4.9 QA Director

The director is one of the highest positions you can get in the QA department. Essentially the role QA director is to direct QA managers. There are more responsibilities than just that, but this is an easy starting point. You could be directing multiple QA managers or even just one. Like other management roles, directors don't spend time in the game or writing bug reports. Directors can report too many high-level positions in a company. These can be directors from other departments or senior-level producers.

Not every company will have a QA director; for instance, small indie studios won't need one, but larger AAA companies with multiple studios worldwide might. You could also have various QA directors, depending on the company's needs. Janel Jolly, a QA Development Director at EA, explains this well.

> *Scalability of the project itself really determines do you need a QA director assigned specifically for that (Game) or if you need a QA director assigned to a studio level.*
>
> *Quote from Janel Jolly*

You could have directors at each studio and one designated global director to whom all studio directors report. Directors are more forward-thinking, considering everything, such as risk management for both the game as well the ethics and standards of the studio. You need to make sure that these are being upheld and ensure accountability.

> *QA director is risk management both for the game quality, as well as upholding the IP that you're working on and keeping the ethics and standards of the studio. So if your standards in the studio have a lot of things towards mental health, then you have to be a protector of your team to ensure that there's no unethical issues are occurring.*
>
> *Quote from Janel Jolly*

Examples of risk management that the director may need to consider could be losing a few senior-level QAs and how to backfill these roles, as well as problems concerning internal builds or software development kits (SDKs) from third parties. Hardware can also be a risk, such as a lack of consoles due to shortages. Directors will also get updates from the producers and other directors about the risks and changes that could impact QA.

Budgeting is another crucial responsibility for directors. Depending on the company, they can directly give the QA department its budget or will provide budgets to development which can then funnel down to QA. At a QA director level, you will provide an approved budget to your QA managers, who will then propose how they will use it. If you get a proposal back or managers request additional funding, the director must get into the specifics. Janel discussed with me some of the reasoning for this.

> *I have to make sure I am doing my due diligence of being an unbiased party and really drilling down into why.*
>
> *Quote from Janel Jolly*

This is because the same questions will be asked to the director when they have justified the use of the budget or increases to other high-level leadership members. By getting these answers, you can present a case to CEOs or other directors and discuss compromises or alternative budgeting. Janel provides an example of how this works in this hypothetical situation.

> *I have already answered the 10 questions that I know they are gonna ask, and I have done that before they even asked it. To prove I have done my homework, I know what I am talking about; we have exhausted this, and these are our options.*
>
> *Quote from Janel Jolly*

Just like with managers, directors have a lot of communication with not only the QA department/s but with the wider company. However, the way directors and managers communicate is different. The best way to explain it is a QA manager's response to changes in development can be more reactive, but as for a director, as we mentioned, it's more forward-thinking discussions.

> *We have to act through the flow of communication, from our testers to their leads, their managers, to the director level. But we do a lot of communication management between development, a lot more than probably a QA manager. QA management can sometimes be a bit reactive. So when a development project is making changes or finishing its features, that flow of information becomes open for test.*
>
> *That goes over to the QA managers, and they kind of handle that. Whereas a QA director, we get to look a bit more forward-thinking because we have to think about, okay, has the staffing on development changed? Because that's gonna affect our ramp and in the next year or in the next financial period, are there any major changes that need to happen?*
>
> *And that sounds a little dry, but it actually does get quite a bit into the design aspect because if development is scaling back or if it's increasing, we have to really ask and drill down into the why. So we know how to properly staff.*
>
> *Quote from Janel Jolly*

Contracts, Different Types of QA Companies, and Wages

2

Now that we have reviewed the different QA roles, let's look at the various contracts available. We will also discuss the different types of QA companies you can work for because there are a few that you might not realise are available as an option. Lastly, a surprisingly tricky section for me to research into, wages!

2.1 FIXED-TERM CONTRACT

Finding job listings for QA testers isn't difficult, as testers are always needed. A lot of QA testing jobs are usually fixed-term contracts. This refers to a worker who is employed by a company for a fixed duration on a contract that both parties sign. These typically range from a minimum of 6-12 months (I don't think I've seen a QA contracts exceeding 12 months.). The positive of working on fixed-term contract is that it can be a good starting point to gain experience, which can help you get other jobs or permanent positions.

These contracts are used because the work of QA is usually in full effect when a game is in the late alpha stage, such as when level/s are in white box or even near the beta stage, where the game is closer to the final product. Standard QA testers aren't required during the pre-production stages. Pre-production is when the game is conceived, concepting different ideas, experimentation with mechanics, and design documentation is still being decided and written up. QA

DOI: 10.1201/9781003314806-2

work does seem to be a good fit within the gig economy due to its reliance on temporary labour during busier periods of game development, such as coming up to a release date.

I genuinely believe that you can build a career within the QA department; however, for job security, you are more likely to have a permanent position if you're a senior or above compared with a standard QA tester role. Don't worry though, as there is hope; when I entered the industry back in 2015, I tried my best to keep up to date with the news surrounding company policies and news. One thing that I have seen is QA jobs are slowly becoming more permanent positions. I have noticed that change in the UK side of the industry; however, in the USA, QA testers are still usually contracted workers but that also seems to be changing. So, there is an inherent risk when starting in QA that you may not have job security. If you have just left university and the sky is your limit, this might not be much of an issue as you may not have many responsibilities. But it is a much higher risk if you're older and may have a family or someone to support.

2.1.1 Fixed-Term Contract Advice

If you are on a fixed-term contract and have around 1 or 2 months left on your contract, APPLY FOR OTHER JOBS! Yes, there is the possibility that your contract may get renewed but remember one thing, nothing is certain. I made this mistake myself; I thought my contract would get renewed; I was one of the few people on the permanent night shift. The shift no one liked to do but had to do for at least 1 week every month. Although my bug count at the time wasn't anything to boast about, I had a decent number of issues reported and completed every smoke document and regression task reasonably. But I was told my contract wasn't renewed a week before it ended. This was a massive disappointment as I was now unemployed, and many other QA jobs I saw advertised at other companies were already filled. So, start looking and applying for more work within that 1–2-month period to ensure some job security.

You might wonder, is it possible to transition to a permanent position? If you want to stay in your current company, opportunities can arise for more permanent positions, depending on the available work. Having fixed-term contract experience will always be beneficial when applying for other QA roles, as you will have the fundamental understanding of the job, making you more employable. I spoke with Naveen Yadav and Darren Eggerton about fixed-term contracts; you can find their advice and insights below:

I mean, a lot of that will just depend on if there is even availability. So if we have no project for them to go on after their contract is over, it can be difficult to renew their contract... If there is, say, one position available, and I have two people that are fighting for it. There are a lot of factors that you'd have to take into account. It's not just who puts out the most bugs; you have to look at the overall picture and what you and your company value. Knowledge gaps can always be filled. Whoever has a better personality, gets on well with the team, and is generally "good" at their job will probably stand out more than someone who is excellent at bug reports or finding issues but doesn't have the right social skills. Someone that is the complete package overall will stand out a lot more for the QA role.

Quote from Naveen Yadav

There's usually some kind of promise of if you stick at it and if you get on well and you are good at the job, we'll make you a permanent position. I think that's valuable to go for, but it's not the only thing you can do, don't take it as a guarantee. I think it's worth looking around for permanent positions as well. If you are not enjoying being fixed-term contract, the uncertainty that comes with that, then you absolutely should try and look around for something that is permanent. But just bear in mind, if you do a good enough job, there is usually a chance of getting a permanent position as well, in my experience.

Quote from Darren Eggerton

2.2 PERMANENT POSITION

This is where you are hired for a role within a company with no set end-date. When you get a permanent position, you will be on your probation period. This is essentially a period set by the company (which can usually range from 3 to 6 months), to assess an employee's performance to ensure they have made the right decision with their recruitment. If an employee is unsuitable for the job, two things can happen, either you are dismissed due to your performance, or you can have an extension on your probation period as a second chance. During your probation period, you will have more meetings with leads or seniors than staff members who have completed their probation. I remember having three meetings with QA leads during my 6-month probation; the first was after my first month, the second was 3 months into the role, and the last meeting was at the end of the probation period to confirm if I had passed.

A permanent position at a company can give you access to benefits such as pension schemes, health, and dental. However, it's important to note that these benefits should also be available to fixed-term workers. This is because fixed-term workers have a legal right to have the same or equivalent benefits as their permanent counterparts. It's worth noting that I am speaking from a UK perspective, so if you are reading this outside of the UK, please look up what legal rights you have as a contract worker in your home country.

2.3 INTERNAL (IN-HOUSE) QA AND EXTERNAL (OUTSOURCE) QA

If you want to get into QA testing, there are two types of companies you can work for: in-house developers and outsource developers. Each has its benefits and drawbacks. Suppose it's your first time looking for industry work. In that case, you may find yourself mainly searching for known developers and assume that all the game-related jobs are in either publishing or development studios. However, outsourcing companies play a substantial role in supporting various aspects of the game development process. You may not hear about them as much, but I guarantee that if you look at the credits of any game, whether it is a big-budget title or indie, at least one outsource studio must have helped support that game.

2.3.1 Internal QA

Internal QA is the QA department within the development or publishing company. So, if you ever wanted to test Fortnite, you would most likely be working at Epic Games. With internal testing, you will only work on titles a specific company is developing. This is something to keep in mind when applying for in-house QA jobs. Some game companies could specialise in particular game genres. Say you applied for a role at Creative Assembly; based on their library of games, you would most likely be working on strategy games. Knowledge and passion for specific genres can be beneficial during the application process. Not all companies will stick with just one genre; companies like Sumo Digital and Team17 have a broad range of genres they work on.

The benefit of being an internal QA is having access to documentation such as game design documents, internal wiki pages (e.g. confluence pages) about every element of the game, a list of console variables, how-to guides, and even internal learning resources. This allows you to familiarise yourself with new content better and refresh your knowledge about the game's inner workings. Being internal can also allow for more opportunities to progress within the company, either in or out of QA. A good company will recognise skills and talents within its workforce and help them grow into their desired development or leadership role.

Getting work for an internal QA role can be a bit more complicated than applying for outsourcing companies, as there is a preference for people with previous experience within the industry. From my experience, many will look for a minimum 1 year worth of experience or have worked on at least one shipped title. Naveen Yadav, QA manager at nDreams, discussed his experience when looking for work.

> *I first looked at studios whose games I enjoy playing. I looked at Blizzard, also play a lot of Rainbow Six, so I looked at Ubisoft, but all of their tester roles need some experience in the industry.*
>
> *Quote from Naveen Yadav*

This isn't to say that it's impossible to get a job without prior experience; if a company offers fixed-term contracts, these can usually be more of an entry-level position that doesn't require previous QA experience.

2.3.2 External QA

Outsourcing is a business practice in which an outside company is hired to perform a service. For example, some companies may want to outsource different development processes such as art, audio/dialogue, motion capture, and even QA. With external QA, you will find that you can work on many different games, from AAA titles to smaller indie games. Naveen Yadav and Andrea Nicolazzo, whom I interviewed for this book, have previously worked for outsourcing QA companies and discussed some of their experiences with me:

> *You won't be stuck on the same project for a long time, you won't get burnt out as much. Your project will keep getting cycled, you have a lot of different clients and a lot of different projects. If you are QA in a studio, you have to test the games they are making.*
>
> *Quote from Naveen Yadav*

With external QA, you will primarily be doing black box testing (you will learn about this term in Chapter 9). You won't have direct communication with the development studio or have access to their internal documentation. You will only have access to builds and possibly their bug-reporting software. External QA companies may be a good starting point to build experience, as their entry requirements for game testing roles are entry-level compared with their internal QA counterparts.

> *We basically have no contact with developers or producers. As testers, we only have contact with our project managers. Our project managers talked to the point of contact of the other company, which can be like a producer, project manager, or lead. All the communication is filtered and delayed a little bit; it makes things a little more difficult.*
>
> *Quote from Andrea Nicolazzo*

When I left university and started looking for work within the industry, I primarily searched for known development studios, not realising that there were other opportunities in outsourcing. You might be wondering what's the best way to find these types of places, now, this might seem like a cop-out answer, but Google is usually the best bet to start with. Later in this book, various sites that could be useful in finding outsourcing companies are mentioned. To get you started, here is a list of a few outsourcing companies (Table 2.1) to help you familiarise yourself with them.

2.4 WAGES IN THE INDUSTRY

Hopefully, the earlier parts of this and the last chapter have helped highlight some of the roles you may be interested in pursuing. But you are probably asking yourself, "Mate, what about the wages". So, like a Simply Red song,

TABLE 2.1   Outsource game companies

COMPANY	DESCRIPTION	WEBSITE
Pole To Win (PTW)	PTW is an outsource development support company with over 35 studios worldwide. They provide a range of support from art, design, localisation, QA, and localisation QA.	www.ptw.com/
Universally Speaking	A UK-based company, one of the longest-running specialist providers. They provide end-to-end QA services for clients.	https://usspeaking.com/
Streamline	Video game outsourcing company with three studios around the world (USA, Colombia, and Malaysia). Day Zero, part of the Streamline media group, focuses on QA and localisation.	www.streamline-mediagroup.com/
Starloop Studios	They are a full-cycle game development solutions company with 14 studios worldwide. They can support many aspects of development from QA to art production, VFX to design.	https://starloopstudios.com/
Keywords Studios	Keywords Studios provided outsource support on various aspects of the game development process with 70+ studios located across 26 countries. They have dedicated studios for different development processes, such as functionality QA and localisation QA.	www.keywordsstudios.com/

we're talking about money. Discussions on salaries are a social taboo that we have been conditioned to accept. For some reason, we can never openly discuss wages with anyone. Job descriptions often use buzzwords like "competitive" or "dependant on experience" to avoid giving people information on actual salaries. You only get that information after successfully completing the application process.

Some countries, such as the USA, are trying to provide more pay transparency, with states Washington, New York, and California already having some form of pay transparency laws. According to a Politico article published on 1 June 2022,[1] there are 10 EU countries with similar pay transparency laws. These have been created to provide more openness to employees to make informed decisions about a job. For instance, is the wage enough to financially support you and your family? This information is vital if you live in cities with high cost of living. Table 2.2 outlines an estimated salary for QA testers.

Please note that the table was created in early 2023 and is a very, VERY rough estimate based on my own research about QA wages. Still, as mentioned earlier, it's not easy to get an accurate range (in fact, the EU one is tough to estimate due to many countries). I got in contact with Skillsearch, an organisation that specialises in game and interactive recruitment. Every year they conduct their "games & interactive salary & satisfaction survey" which provides information on not just salaries but points of interests within the industry, such as four-day workweek discussions. They were lovely enough to provide me with a set of QA specific data they got from their survey. Figure 2.1 is my reproduction of their average salary data chart. This hopefully gives you a more accurate picture and insight into average salaries not just in the QA hierarchy but globally as well.

It's also worth noting that wages can vary depending on the region. For example, salaries in the north of England may be slightly lower compared with the south (e.g. London) due to the higher cost of living. The more experience you have can also increase your salary. As the years go on, your country's wages may increase due to inflation and through legislation, so if you're reading this book in 100 years, you might wonder, "Why isn't the table in republic credits". Well, it's because this section will get dated quickly.

Historically, QA jobs in the game industry have been the lowest-paid jobs in games. The lowest end of the pay scale can be minimum wage (for a regular game tester) to just above that. Of course, if you move up the hierarchy, pay increases, but there is still a pay gap compared with senior-level jobs in other departments. So why is a base game tester role paid less than their software testing counterparts? One reason could be software testing requires more technical knowledge (in fact, many companies have an ISTQB (International Software Testing Qualifications Board) qualification as a requirement). I personally don't believe that game testing is lesser than software testing. In fact, many people have transitioned from game testing to software testing, as there are many similarities between the two jobs. As mentioned in Chapter 1, there are technical roles within games QA. There is an assumption that games QA is just an entry-level position and doesn't require much skill to do the job as compared with software testing; however, a good QA tester is worth their weight in gold. Having someone experienced who can effectively find and report bugs will save developers a lot of time and be of great support. Janel spoke about issues someone can face when trying to make QA a career in games.

TABLE 2.2   VERY rough estimates of QA salaries (I tried my best, honestly)

JOB ROLE	UK SALARY RANGE	EU SALARY RANGE	US SALARY RANGE
Game tester	£20,000–21,000	€27,000–37,000	$21,000–34,000
Senior	£22,000–25,000	€37,000–46,000	$27,000–38,000
Lead	£24,000–30,000	€50,000–60,000	$50,000–58,000
Manager	£30,000–35,000	€60,000–73,000	$54,000–110,000

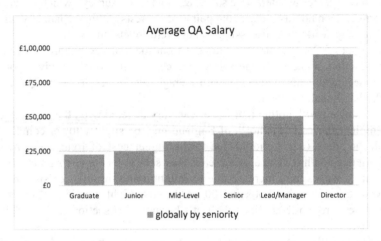

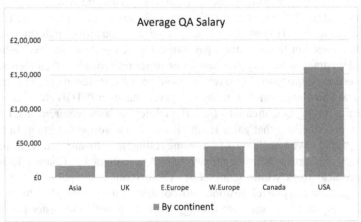

FIGURE 2.1   Average QA salary data from Skillsearch QA survey report 2023.

> *Building a career in QA is so rare and difficult. Mainly due to the pay, there's a ceiling. So, if you are now supporting a family, so you got married, and you're gonna have kids. This job you have in QA might not be financially supportive for your family now, or say you wanna buy a home, you know you're not able to make enough to make that happen. But you know that "Hey, if I go to development, I can do similar stuff and get paid even better and maybe even get full-time".*
>
> *Quote from Janel Jolly*

The game industry as a whole doesn't pay as well compared with their software industry peers. I understand this is a huge sweeping generalisation as many companies pay very well, but there is a general consensus that low pay is an issue within the industry. You can find online the UK game developer salaries spreadsheet, created by several industry workers to help encourage more pay transparency. So look at that spreadsheet, and you'll see what the pay situation looks like (at the very least from a UK point of view). UNI Global Union published a report in June 2022, which included a survey on workplace issues; low pay was the most cited issue, with 66% of survey respondents reporting this as an issue. It's worth noting that only 512 workers in the industry were questioned for the survey, which is a small sample size compared with the size of some companies' workforce. Still, it helps to identify areas of concern and improvement. And according to QA data provided by Skillsearch, 17.5% of QA responses to their survey put salary as most important aspect of work.

NOTE

1   Paola Tamma. "Does Gender Pay Transparency Work?" Published on June 1, 2022. Available at: https://www.politico.eu/article/pay-transparency-pay-off-gender-gap/

Education and Mentoring 3

This chapter will discuss ways to learn about the game development pipelines, procedures, and routes to expand your knowledge. The first section will look into formal education, from discussions on vocational and degree-level courses. Please remember that I will try to be as international as possible with the formal education parts. Most of my experience and knowledge are geared towards the UK educational system due to my previous jobs. Listing all the different courses and educational systems in every continent would be a book in and of itself. So, I won't be able to go into in-depth discussions with European or various North American systems, but I will attempt to discuss some of these.

3.1 FURTHER EDUCATION

If you are a UK student, then further education (FE) can allow you to explore courses on a wide range of vocations. Many FE colleges around the UK offer some form of a game development course; these courses can range from level 2 (equivalent to GCSE) to level 3 (equivalent to A-levels). Suppose you wish to go through the educational route. In that case, a level 3 games development course is ideal as many UK residents can partake in a level 3 course with no added cost (unless you already completed one). It will allow you to learn the fundamentals of game development. You will not be a specialist as that would require you to pursue a degree where you can specialise in a specific subject. But you will learn the basic principles of industry software such as game engines like Unity and Unreal and understand the development process and pipeline. You can even study art tools such as various 3D modelling packages like Maya or 3DS Max, commonly used in the industry.

You may wonder why you would want to do an FE course. One of the reasons could be financial. Some people may not be able to afford a high-end gaming PC which can go into the 1,000s. So learning from home could be off

 DOI: 10.1201/9781003314806-3

the table, so FE colleges and universities are a great way for people to access hardware that would allow them to study and learn.

From discussions with game development professors in the USA, there does not seem to be a system similar to the UK's FE options. I spoke with two game development professors in the USA, Jack Mamais, professor of game design at SCAD, and Amanda Lange, former professor at the Kutztown University of Pennsylvania, to learn about game courses over in the USA and general education system. There does not seem to be a similar system for FE, continuing education or advanced placement is probably the closest comparison to FE in the USA. Most students in the USA, after achieving their high school diploma, move to a university for a degree in their preferred field.

When I was in high school, they did have the possibility of doing a vocational school for your last two years of high school. But I think the more common path is just to go straight from high school to university. I don't think it's very common to learn game dev in high school. There's the occasional computer science student that I get that has learned computer science in high school. Sometimes there's computer science classes in high school, but generally speaking, they don't know about it unless they've done it as a hobby on their own.

Quote from Amanda Lange

Generally, people won't start any kind of real game design until they get to college. So, there's really no prep; as far as I know, there's no game vocational prep. You come to college and start working on it; you can do stuff on your own. There's no prep school for college and games, as far as I know. I mean, that could change tomorrow.

Quote from Jack Mamais

3.2 APPRENTICESHIPS

With an apprenticeship, you are employed to do a job while completing a formal qualification. In addition, you will spend at least 1 day in a college or university studying towards a technical qualification. Apprenticeships can range from level 3 qualifications (GCSE equivalent) to level 7 (master's equivalent).

Apprenticeships in the game industry were, at one point, pretty much non-existent. Graduate schemes or internships were the closest you could get to something like apprenticeships. Into Games did a report on the state of apprenticeships within the UK games industry, which goes over the benefits of implementing these in a company and providing suggestions for types of apprenticeship roles that companies can offer from technical roles like programming to other roles ranging from marketing to HR (https://intogames.org/news/into-games-releases-the-uk-games-apprenticeship-2021/). As the years go on, it will be interesting to see if companies will start to implement more junior and apprentice positions, but right now it's a waiting game to see how the industry responds. However, there is some progress already happening in this area. Some companies, like XR Games in Leeds in 2022, began to offer a level 7 game programmer apprenticeship. Sumo Digital in Sheffield also provides similar apprenticeships for programmers.

3.3 HIGHER EDUCATION

Higher education (HE) is your standard university degree level course, from undergraduate up to a master's degree and even Ph.D. If you are considering going down the university route, it's important to figure out what interests you. Are you interested in animation? Do you want to create the art for the game? Do you want to be a programmer, or designer, or even work in visual effects? By the time you get to university, you need to think about where you want to be in 5-6 years.

The number of games-related courses has steadily increased worldwide as the industry continues to grow. In 2018, the Higher Education Statistics Agency (HESA) in the UK provided figures showing that the number of people studying games-related courses was increasing. You can see a breakdown of the student number in Table 3.1. You can see that the numbers increased by 129% for design courses, followed by design and graphics courses at 124%, with graphics courses increasing by 111% between the academic years of 2014/15 and 2016/17.

In February 2019, HESA provided updated statistics on the number of students graduated in game-related subjects for 2018/19 (see Table 3.2). Although there is a slight dip in student numbers between 2016/17 and 2017/18 (a difference of around 1.9%), you can see that it is a consent trend of more students wanting to learn and study games.

So why am I telling you these stats? Well, it's to show you how many graduates are in the same boat as you. So, if you're looking to go down the university route, take caution and ensure that you're going to a university that

TABLE 3.1 Statistics of video game students

ACADEMIC YEAR	NUMBER OF QUALIFIERS IN COMPUTER GAME DESIGN	NUMBER OF QUALIFIERS IN COMPUTER GAMES GRAPHICS	NUMBER OF QUALIFIERS IN COMPUTER GAME DESIGN AND GAMES GRAPHICS
2014/15	240	45	285
2015/16	240	60	485
2016/17	550 (129%)	95 (111%)	640 (124%)

Source: https://tiga.org/news/video-games-student-numbers-skyrocket

TABLE 3.2 Number of graduates in computer games

ACADEMIC YEAR	NUMBER OF QUALIFIERS IN COMPUTER GAMES SUBJECTS
2012/13	595
2013/14	625
2014/15	690
2015/16	900
2016/17	1,290
2017/18	1,265
2018/19	1,380

Source: https://tiga.org/news/number-of-computer-games-graduates-at-a-seven-year-high

works for you, as not all universities are the same. Some may have games in the title, but the content doesn't reflect what you want to learn. So, it's important to ensure that you vet courses before going on them, as you are taking a big financial risk. Ideally, you want to go onto a course that is accredited or affiliated with an industry body like TIGA or Ukie in the UK. If you find a course that isn't affiliated, but you are interested in, it could be worth reaching out to games alumni who have done the course, and getting their feedback to see if it worked for them.

You can use open days or taster sessions to help make the right decision. First, it's important to learn more about the university. If you can talk to any of the tutors, ask about their background and relevant industry experience, what software they use, the course material, how up to date they are with current industry trends, and what opportunities and events students can participate in. Some universities will tack on a few modules that cover game development and try to sell that as a games course to get people to join. Even for the ones that are specialists, one of the issues there is that it's not specialised enough. Take art for instance, if you do a university games art course, you could cover multiple subjects, from characters, environment art to concept art. Each of these is a specialism in its own right, so trying to learn all three of these will mean that you might end up being a jack of all trades of an artist but a master of none. You might not even have the chance to specialise and dedicate your time to one specific area you want to go into unless you're using your free time.

Not every university will be accredited by an industry body. Still, some can have connections with the industry through contacts with companies or industry organisations, for example, in the UK, Into Games, Grads in Games, or even game networks like Game Republic in the north of England. Courses with these connections can help with work experience opportunities, attend talks, and be featured in student showcases. Take Game Republic, every year, they do a student showcase where educational members can show their students' best work to industry professionals.

Now depending on location and university, these options might not be available. Now this is where a student membership to the International Game Developers Association (IGDA) could come in handy. In case you haven't heard of IGDA, it's the world's largest non-profit organisation for game developers. Anyone who creates games, whether you're indie development, work in an AAA studio, or a games student, you can be eligible for membership. If you are a games student, I highly recommend looking into it, as its various benefits can help you expand your network and learning. For example, you will be able to get discounts on software, industry events, as well as access to IGDA resources. As a student, you can also benefit from the student portfolio, which will help get your name out there for people to see and you can gain early access to job postings. They also help with applying for jobs, but one I think you can benefit the most from is their global mentorship programme, which lasts for 3 months and will pair you with a mentor working within the industry and an IGDA member. Being able to get one-on-one mentoring with someone who works in the industry is a great way to gain insight into how the industry works and learn how to make yourself stand out when searching for work. Tarja Porkka-Kontturi, who I interviewed for this book, is on the board of directors of IGDA, and I asked her about student membership.

Here in Finland, we encourage students to join IGDA in the early stage, so they can network, create those connections, and take all the support they can. So, their career would have a good start, and they wouldn't feel like they are confused or alone. But we believe that community

> *support is crucial, and we invite everyone to join from the early stages*
> *of their journey. And that's usually when you start to study. Of course,*
> *not everyone studies game development. They may end up in the industry*
> *from other routes.*
>
> *Quote from Tarja Porkka-Kontturi*

Not many companies will hold degrees in high regard when it comes down to applying for jobs. Employers want to see that you can do the job, which is why many industry peers, experts, and veterans will say that a portfolio is the most valuable thing to have as it can showcase just what you are capable of, as both Jack and Amanda discuss. In terms of QA testing, having a portfolio isn't a requirement but it can be a plus to showcase that you aren't just a person that likes to play games but one who actively learns and creates them. It can be helpful later if you want to apply for a more technical QA role or embedded position. A degree may benefit you as it may boost your application over another candidate. It may also open up opportunities to work abroad due to your specialist skills (although this might not be applicable for QA roles abroad, as you will read about soon).

> *You don't need to have a degree to be a game developer; you just need*
> *to know how to do it. I think game development is a field where it is way*
> *more portfolio based than it is based on what degree you have or what*
> *your degree is in. They just wanna know what your skill set is.*
>
> *Quote from Amanda Lange*

> *As far as an employer looking for a person, if you had a degree in bad*
> *work and had you great work and no degree. They're gonna hire you*
> *with the great work every time, the degree is gonna be less. But if they*
> *were on the fence about you and they saw that you did not graduate, but*
> *you went there and stopped there, that might give them pause to say,*
> *"Why didn't you finish your degree?" Typically I would say it's abso-*
> *lutely beneficial for them to get that diploma in hand.*
>
> *Quote from Jack Mamais*

However, going down the traditional education route can be a good start for some people to understand the game development process and get access to industry-standard software and hardware. In addition, if you go to a good university with connections to the industry, you can gain access to events, speakers, and maybe connect with alumni. Perhaps you need that dedicated time to upskill yourself in your craft, so having the time to study, experiment, and learn in a place with dedicated facilities can be a benefit of going to university, as Amanda discusses.

The lessons you learn in the classroom, particularly the access to mentorship and software. Cause some software is super expensive; art software is super expensive, I think that's very beneficial. The degree itself, eh? As long as you build a good portfolio. When I was an undergrad, I saw people that half-assed their classes. I'll tell students this upfront; I'll be honest, they half-assed their classes and get C's and kind of coast, but they were working on really strong portfolio pieces as a side project and not so concerned about their grades in the class.

And those are the students that got hired at studios. So it's not really about the degree; it's about the stuff you make while you're doing the degree. And if you graduate with a game dev degree and you made a couple of really good games like prototypes, or you made the art for a game, or you made the UI for a really good game. You have that piece to show an employer and say; this is what I'm capable of. And they'll say, great, even if you don't graduate. You could learn that all on your own and have those portfolio pieces. Would you have the same access to instructors and mentorship? Some people just need the discipline. I know I do; I'm very unfocused. Personal projects I do a lot of them don't always get finished. But if I have somebody breathing down my neck, like, this has a deadline, I'm gonna get it done. So the benefits of school are, to me, intangible rather than It's the paperwork, which doesn't matter.

Quote from Amanda Lange

If you want to study abroad because you saw a fantastic game design school, there is another risk you must manage: visa. Janel, the QA director at EA, who also taught at Vancouver Film School, has explained the importance of getting a work visa or, at the very least, a student visa. A visa will allow you to stay in a country for an extended period of time. You will need to research the country you are in and see the limits of student visas. If you are looking to get work within a country you are studying in, your first job will most likely be in QA, as that's where many people will get their start. However, because a traditional QA testing role is mostly an entry-level position, the chances of getting work visas for these roles are slim to none.

> *getting a job in the gaming industry can be hard. More than likely, your first job in the gaming industry is going to be through QA, and QA does not give you work visas on a tester level. Unless you are very, very senior.*
>
> *Quote from Janel Jolly*

3.4 GRADUATE SCHEMES AND INTERNSHIPS

A benefit of being a student or a recent graduate is that you may be applicable for graduate schemes/internships at a studio. Many AAA game studios offer graduate placements for people doing a placement year as part of their university program, are in their final year of studies, or just recently graduated (usually within the last 12 months). However, the current issue when writing this book is that if you do not have a formal education, there are few internship opportunities for you. You can use the information in Chapter 5 to help you find companies; maybe some of the studios you find during your search will have internships available. It's worth having some work to demonstrate and showcase if you apply for internships. You need to prove that you have a fundamental knowledge of particular disciplines, such as art or design, to work within a company. As mentioned before, a portfolio will be beneficial here as well.

3.5 ISTQB QUALIFICATIONS

Although not a requirement for QA games testing, certification from International Software Testing Qualifications Board (ISTQB) could provide more opportunities within QA in both games and software testing (if you wanted to change industries). An ISTQB qualification will allow you to learn different methodologies and specialisms within software testing. You could be a tester who understands agile methodologies or specialise in other areas of software testing, such as automation and even managerialism. The only downside to this is you have to pay to get ISTQB training and qualification, so you will have to do the leg work and find accredited instructors who can educate you and sign you up for exams. Prices will vary from provider to provider. It won't be cheap, so make sure you have some spending money if you want to get this qualification (I saw some foundation courses costing around £800, and higher-level courses can go over £1,000). You can find accredited trainers and exam providers through the ISTQB website. If you get a job as a QA tester, it might be worth approaching management about getting access to these courses (that's if they have the budget for staff development).

3.6 ALTERNATIVE WAYS OF LEARNING

For many people, the traditional education route may seem to be the only way to learn skills needed within the industry. But that isn't the case anymore; there is a wealth of knowledge online that can help you develop your technical skills. It's important to note that you may learn different techniques or pipelines because anyone can upload videos or courses online. So be mindful of the age of videos and courses to ensure that you are not learning something outdated.

3.6.1 YouTube

YouTube isn't just used to watch 2 hours' worth of cat videos but can help your self-development. Many educational channels focus on game development, from learning how to model if you wish to be an artist to level design. But as mentioned at the start, it's worth taking some of the advice and skills learning with a pinch of salt because anyone can upload videos onto the site. Try using channels that have up-to-date tutorials for software you wish to learn. The official Unity and Unreal channels can have tutorials to learn the fundamentals of their game engines and even have examples of games you can make. Some other channels I would recommend are GDC, Game Makers Toolkit, Extra Credit, Ask Gamedev, and lastly NoClip – Video Game Documentaries (if you want to learn more behind the scenes of games and the people behind them).

3.6.2 Code Coven

This industry-focused classroom and accelerator provides a friendly and inclusive learning environment for all its students. Their mission is to develop marginalised genders' skills to help them succeed in the game industry. Students will be able to learn game-making in Unity and Unreal. All the courses they offer are part-time, online based, and, best of all, free! You can learn more by visiting their website: https://codecoven.co/.

3.6.3 Udemy

It is an online learning platform where people can purchase courses on any topic they wish to learn about. There are many courses around game development which could be a good starting point to learn 3D modelling, design, or game engines. Anyone can sign up as an instructor and upload courses to the site. You may want to check out course reviews or even check out the instructor's social media, such as LinkedIn, to ensure they have the relevant experience to deliver a course. You can check out more on their site: www.udemy.com/.

3.6.4 Pluralsight

Pluralsight is a site that provides skill assessments, learning support on getting certification, and various online courses for tech industry such as software development, cybersecurity, and even the creative sector, like games. You will have to subscribe (either monthly or yearly) to the site; they also offer standard or premium subscriptions. You can see what courses they offer here: www.plur alsight.com/product/skills.

3.6.5 LinkedIn Learning

This is an online educational platform that is part of the LinkedIn platform. LinkedIn provides courses on developing or up-levelling your skills, such as creative skills, software, production, or business skills. After finishing a course, you can get a certificate to prove you have completed it. Now these alone won't get you work in the industry but can hold some value as it showcases that you have taken the time to work on your personal development. Similar to Pluralsight, users have to subscribe to the service to gain access to these resources. You can learn more about the service here: www.linkedin.com/learning/.

3.7 MENTORSHIPS AND SCHEMES

Many people in the games industry want to help others break into it. However, approaching people or groups at an event can be pretty intimidating. And although it's great to get a few minutes to talk to someone and get some advice, it can be better to have someone there more consistently to help you through your game development journey. That is where mentorships and graduate schemes can help you, so check out the list below and see which ones you think will apply.

3.7.1 IGDA Global Mentorship Programme

We have already discussed this earlier, but just to recap, this is a 3-month mentorship for IGDA members. Because IGDA has different chapters world-wide, this mentorship can be more accessible to international readers. The sessions can be remote, so don't worry about having to be there in-person. You should aim for at least five interactions, lasting a minimum of 30 minutes.

3.7.2 Xbox Mentoring

This new initiative by Xbox provides one-on-one coaching opportunities to help those looking to kick start their game industry career. Like with the IGDA, the programme is 3 months long, but as it is one-on-one, you will have time and space to work closely with your mentor for them to tailor their help and advice to whatever your goals are. It's worth noting that Xbox mentorship is currently active in the following territories: US, UK, DACH, France, ANZ, Japan, and Korea.

3.7.3 Limit Break Mentorship

Founded in 2019, Limit Break has grown into one of the UK's biggest game industry mentorship programmes. It has various sponsorships from many game industry organisations. Their main goal is to help support people in marginalised communities such as LGBTQ+ and POC (people of colour). It is worth mentioning that Limit Break is mainly used for people inside the industry looking to develop themselves further or for people outside of games industry looking to get into the industry, so it isn't really for students. However, if you are graduating close to the time the mentorship starts or recently graduated, then you can be eligible for the mentorship programme.

3.7.4 BAME in Games

Also known as BiG, this is an advocacy group founded in 2016 and dedicated to promoting and improving diversity within the games industry, such as encouraging POC to pursue careers in both video games and the wider entertainment industry. One of the initiatives they have is their Games Digital Mentorship Programme which is a free programme for marginalised ethnicities to sign up as a mentee and get paired with established figures in the industry.

3.7.5 Into Games

Into Games is a non-profit organisation that helps people find their way into the games industry. The contents are usually geared more towards students but can be used by anyone. In addition, you can request mentors within the industry who can help and guide you. A wealth of resources here that can help you search for training sessions, jobs, information on upcoming career events, and breakdowns of different job roles with interviews from people within the industry.

3.7.6 Grads in Games

Grads in Games help graduates transition from being students into professional industry jobholders. They can provide resources to help you develop yourself, but they also host programmes such as the Games Careers Week, which hosts talks and network opportunities. They also offer game development challenges as well. Taking part in these is a great way to get yourself some exposure and network with industry professionals, as Grads in Games have many partners and sponsors from large AAA and independent companies who help to judge contestants. You could potentially put in your CV that you participated in these competitions, and it would be an even bigger highlight if you win.

3.7.7 Women in Games International (WIGI)

Founded in 2005, WIGI is a non-profit organisation that promotes equality and diversity within the industry. It provides various resources for those who identify as women, femme-identifying, and non-binary professionals in the games industry. On their website, there are multiple programmes, such as mentorship, that you can sign up for.

Community, Networking, and Events

4

You may have had the unfortunate experience where you applied for a job that appears to be entry-level, but you get turned down due to your lack of "experience". It's that awful loop of you needing a job to gain experience, but you need the experience to get a job. As a result, you may need to think about alternative ways to acquire skills and knowledge. Participating in the development community can help make your applications stand out and potentially increase your employment opportunities. This can be in the form of game jams, being a part of the modding community, to even networking.

4.1 USABILITY TESTING AND PLAYTESTING

One way you can gain experience in a games company without having a job is to partake in usability testing, otherwise known as playtesting. If you're unfamiliar with this term, companies will host sessions with players to playtest and provide crucial feedback on games, usually unleased games. Playtesting/ usability testing provides developers with information about the user experience. Developers need to know how the game feels. Is it intuitive? Is it easy to understand? Is it confusing for the players? All this information is vital and can only be gathered through usability testing.

Sometimes these tests are done internally using the QA department, but game development studios and publishers will host playtesting sessions for players to attend. There are also third-party companies that will host usability

DOI: 10.1201/9781003314806-4

labs in conjunction with a games company. If you partake in such testing, make sure that you provide comprehensive and well-thought-out feedback to help developers. If you've done multiple playtest sessions for a particular company or numerous companies, you can add this to your CV, which could help you stand out from people who haven't.

4.2 COMMUNITY BUG REPORTS

Another way to gain testing experience would be actively participating in bug reporting for existing games. You can submit bugs directly to a game's website, forum rooms, or dedicated community websites. Some games may even have the option to report issues in-game, for example, encountering a crash. In a game, you will usually be asked to submit a crash report to assist developers in reproducing the issue. This can be somewhat challenging with a game already released because the company's internal QA would have picked up on many of these issues. So, when you are playing the game, you are experiencing a mostly bug-free environment. That doesn't mean there will be no bugs. It just means that they might be a little bit harder to find. Live service games are constantly changing and evolving, so bugs can be a bit more plentiful compared with a single-player experience. You can read Chapter 9 to see how a bug report should be structured. But to quickly summarise, make sure that you provide as much detail as possible to a developer. Provide supplementary materials such as screenshots and videos to allow developers to reproduce your issue easily. If your report is structured well enough, you can use it as an example to potential employers when you apply for a QA job.

4.3 GAME JAMS

These are events where people come together to make a video game. Usually, participants have to create prototype games traditionally based on a specific theme within a certain amount of time. These are great ways of injecting new ideas into the game development community, inspiring others and encouraging you to think creatively and develop your problem-solving abilities, especially under the time pressure that comes with game jams. The time given for a jam can vary from organisation to organisation. Some are usually one or two days long, some could take a week, like Adventure Game Jam, or even half a day. These are great ways of getting involved with the community. Everyone is encouraged to join; you don't have to have experience doing it, although it can be a plus. Tarja, whom I quoted in Chapter 3, is also the director of community engagement for Global Game Jam. She has discussed with me the benefits of participating in a game jam.

> *Whatever the reason is, people often hesitate too much, just go for it; that's the most important rule. Don't be afraid, go in and see what happens and if you don't have any skills before you join, you will, after you finished with the jam.*
>
> *Quote from Tarja Porkka-Kontturi*

Taking part in a jam is a great way to network. You will meet many people, from hobbyists to industry professionals (whether it be indie or AAA). Working with people from different backgrounds will help you grow your confidence in not just in the development process but also in growing connections with other people due to your love of making games.

> *Its an efficient way to start networking, even if you never did networking before and feel kind out of water. Because this one common thing connects everyone, and it's games; it's love for games and making them. It's the perfect way to start your career or try to get your foot in the door. And there's so many success stories, people who got their first job because of the game jam.*
>
> *Quote from Tarja Porkka-Kontturi*

If you want to participate in a game jam, you can do it alone if you have the skillset to create a game or join a team. Some people will assemble teams of friends or work colleagues before the jam starts. Maybe you want to be a part of a team. You could do the same, but if you don't know anyone with specific skills to help make a game, you may want to try reaching out to others. Many game jams will have a community that you can get involved with. There could be a call out from other teams looking for people with specific skills, or you could try talking to community members to see if you can work together or join other groups.

There's usually some platform used for communication, and it's usually Discord cause that's the gamers' platform. There's often places for people to do a shoutout like, "Hey, I'm this and this, my skills are this and this". Or if you don't feel confident enough to announce you have some skillset, you can say, "I would love to learn this or that skill". You can even announce, "I will do anything if you help me", or "Would there be someone who would like to mentor me". I've seen that happen, and people have been really open to taking newcomers and helping them.

You don't have to end up doing the game jam alone. You can just jump in Discord or whatever platform that's used and introduce yourself and then either say what you could do or ask: Is there something I could do? Someone maybe get left alone, but mostly these are successful ways when you go and introduce yourself. I understand that people can be really shy. It can feel like a huge thing to just introduce yourself to some strangers. But in my experience, for example, the Global Game Jam community has been really warm.

Quote from Tarja Porkka-Kontturi

Participating in a game jam will involve you in the development process. Being able to experiment with different ideas and seeing something come together in a short amount of time is a great experience. Plus, you can add it to your CV or cover letter as it showcases that you've been participating within the community. It's also great motivation to learn new skills. There are so many game engines that are very easily accessible. Maybe you're not great at programming, so you might do visual scripting in game engines like Unreal Engine, Unity's visual scripting, Scratch, or Construct. Table 4.1 lists some sites you can check if you want to take part in a game jams.

4.4 NETWORKING AND EVENTS

Networking is vital to pretty much any industry, not just in games. It allows you to take this faceless corporation and humanise it as you interact with people who work behind the scenes to bring a product to life. Networking is an excellent way to learn about that company's work culture (without breaking NDA). You can get advice on your CVs, cover letters, and portfolios. You

TABLE 4.1 Game jam sites you can visit

NAME	DESCRIPTION	WEBSITE
Global Game Jam	This is the biggest game jam in the world. It's a 48-hour game jam that usually takes place in January, with registration around November and December.	globalgamejam.org/
Game jams on itch.io	Itch.io is an open marketplace for independent developers to sell their content. Itch.io allows people to host and participate in game jams.	itch.io/jams
Indie Game Jams	Indie Game Jam is a website listing all the available game jams worldwide.	www.indiegamejams.com
Adventure Game Jam	This is a 2-week game jam where participants must create an adventure game. This can be visual novels, classic point-and-click games, or text-based adventures.	advjam.com/

can even find out what they're looking for in a candidate. Attending events is a great way to meet people who work in the industry. There are many networking opportunities and showcase events throughout the world that you can attend.

When you think of events, you may automatically think of the more consumer-focused ones, such as E3 or Gamescom. Consumer events are where the general public and industry professionals can play the newest and upcoming games on various platforms. These events will have multiple booths from companies and publishers showing off their titles, usually manned by company members. Events such as EGX can also host various talks, panels, and career advice. This can greatly benefit someone wanting to start out in the industry.

While these events are a great way to meet developers, you may want to expand your horizon towards more conference-based events. These would be events like the Games Developer Conference (GDC) or Develop:Brighton. The focus is on educating and sharing ideas and experiences with others. Conferences like Develop will discuss a wide range of topics, from discussions on game design case studies, technical talks, to conversations on the latest hot topics surrounding the game industry. However, it's not just the talks that are important but the exhibitions and booths. These will allow you to meet recruiters from game companies and learn what they are looking for in a candidate.

These events cost money, not just the tickets but travel and accommodation, so make sure you factor this in when deciding to attend events. There are many game industry events going on throughout the year. Some of these could be very close to home, so you don't have to travel to different countries to meet developers. Check out this list of just some of the events that could be worth attending.

4.4.1 EGX – London (UK)

This is a trade fair for video games that takes place in October. It's primarily consumer focused with various AAA to indie titles to play. The EGX theatre also has talks from industry professionals about various topics (www.egx.net/).

4.4.2 E3 – Los Angeles (USA)

E3 was one of the biggest trading shows in the game industry, where many of the biggest game announcements happen. In the past, it has only been for industry professionals and the press, but since 2017 it has been open to the public. The event takes place in mid to late July (www.e3expo.com/).

It's worth noting that last E3 event was in 2021 (which was Online due to the pandemic). Since then the event has been canceled numerous time due to lack of interest from various publishers and game industry business. May be this event will return in some way in the future.

4.4.3 Gamescom – Cologne (Germany)

A trade fair in Cologne takes place in mid- to late August. Like E3, there are many game announcements alongside the exhibits for consumers to play games, and there is also a business area for developers to network (www. gamescom.global/).

4.4.4 Animex – Middlesbrough (UK)

Animex is an annual festival for animation, VFX, and games, providing various talks from these three industries. Teesside University hosts the event; the event doesn't really have specific months when it runs, so it's best to check out their social media or keep an eye out on their website for announcements (animex.tees.ac.uk/).

4.4.5 Yorkshire Games Festival – Bradford (UK)

Yorkshire Games Festival is a weeklong event with various events from the northern game showcase. It includes family events and two days of game talks from industry professionals with opportunities to participate in networking events with all the speakers. The event takes place in the first week of February (www.scienceandmediamuseum.org.uk/whats-on/yorksh ire-games-festival).

4.4.6 PAX Events (PAX East, PAX West, PAX AUS) – Seattle, Boston (USA), Melbourne (Australia)

Created by Penny Arcade, this is a celebration of gaming and it's community. It is more consumer focused but provides talks from people within the industry. There are many versions of PAX that you can attend, so it's best to check out their site for more info (www.paxsite.com/).

4.4.7 Nordic Game – Malmö (Sweden)

This is one of the leading game conferences in Europe that takes place around mid- to late May. They host various talks, have exhibitors from many game companies, and support studios with industry stalls. The event also hosts online showcases and discussions and has discord for those unable to attend in person (conf.nordicgame.com/).

4.4.8 WASD – London (UK)

A game event with a good mix of AAA and indie games. Able to attend talks from developers, it takes place in early April. There are also WASD Careers that focus on connecting education and industry with recruitment areas, networking events, and student showcases (www.wasdlive.com/).

4.4.9 Develop:Brighton – Brighton (UK)

It is a conference, expo, and networking event that takes place in mid-July. The talks cost money, but the expo day is free to attend and will allow you to meet recruiters and visit company stalls to learn more about them and what jobs they have going (www.developconference.com/).

4.4.10 Hamburg Games Conference – Hamburg (Germany)

This event takes place in early March. The conference usually has a particular theme which all keynotes and talks will be based around. Alongside the talks, there are networking events to attend (www.gamesconference.com/).

4.4.11 Games Job Fair – Helsinki (Finland), Online

A hybrid event that allows studios to actively look for new talent to recruit. The event hosts challenges, workshops, and lets you network and discuss jobs and requirements with studios and their recruiters (gamesjobfair.com/).

The list above is just a small handful of events; if I were to list every single industry event, this book would probably double in size, so if you are looking for events near you, then feel free to use the following sites to help you find the events:

- www.gameconfguide.com/
- www.gamesindustry.biz/network/events

4.5 LOCAL MEETUPS

Aside from larger events, you can also attend local developer meetups. These are typically social events where people interested in games or work within the industry come together and socialise (usually meeting up at a bar or café). These small events are informal and are a great way for local or regional developers to catch up with friends or meet one another.

These meetups usually occur once a month (this can vary from event to event) and will have a designated location for everyone to meet up. Some will have specific days of the month and certain times. Take my home county of West Yorkshire, there is the Leeds Games Toast on the last Tuesday of every month.

The benefit of these networking events is that they are relatively local to you (depending where you live). You don't have to break the bank to travel to large metropolitan cities or buy a ticket to attend. Everyone is welcome, and because of the informal nature of these meet-ups, it can be easier to chat with people without the intimidating backdrop of a large conference.

If you are from the UK, you can use ukiepedia.ukie.org.uk/, a site maintained by Ukie hosting various industry resources and support. If you search for "Meetups" on this site, you will find a list of local meets nationwide.

Sadly most of my knowledge of these smaller-sized meetups is more UK-based, but sites like www.meetup.com/ can be a great way to search for any informal game development meets happening near you. But don't worry if you can't make it to these in-person events because you can become a part of plenty of online communities.

4.6 ONLINE COMMUNITIES

Social media platforms are a great way to connect with people, get into health discussions, heated arguments, or both!

4.6.1 Discord

This is a free voice, chat, and video app that allows users to be part of different communities by joining servers. These servers are generally centred around a particular topic. You can only participate in a server after being invited into one, as most servers are private. It's prevalent among gamers as many official and unofficial gaming communities have servers centred around particular games or companies. Discord is a great way to connect with other gamers. Still, you can use it to network with various industry professionals as there are many communities you can be a part of, such as IGDA Discord, Game Dev Network, and BAME in Game.

4.6.2 Twitter (Also Known as X)

Everyone's favourite place for doom and gloom, Twitter allows anyone to send out short messages known as tweets for people to read.[1] Because tweets are limited to a maximum of 280 characters (I am old enough to remember when it used to be 140), it's easy to digest; you can scroll through and scan many tweets at a glance.

Don't just follow game companies. Follow people who work on them. It's a great way to learn about opportunities such as jobs and be informed about events people attend or promote. You will also learn about any hot topics currently being discussed in the industry.

Twitter has been very inconsistent since late 2022, with Elon Musk taking on the role of CEO. There have been many policies and changes to the platform which have been controversial, to put it nicely. For instance, Twitter Blue and removing blue check marks for prominent figureheads, making it a pain to tell the difference between a well-known developer you want to follow and someone who wasted $8 to appear important or worse to be an imposter.

4.7 NETWORKING TIPS AND ADVICE

Try to go into conversation with the intent to make a new connection or new friend. Introduce yourself, talk about what you do, and ask the same to the person you are talking to. Ask questions, and you will quickly find something in common that helps take away some of your nerves. If you are nervous, try taking a friend with you; that has always made me feel more comfortable. When I attend networking events alone, I feel anxious and unsure of myself, which can sometimes hinder me from meeting someone new. Don't forget to swap contact details such as emails, numbers, or even social media like a Twitter handle. That way, you can continue talking to people after the networking event.

When networking online, try to be aware of a few things: your communication skills, specifically any text messages you send via social media, emails, or even phone texts. Sometimes what we write down can be misconstrued, so be mindful of what and how you write. If you are on a call with other people, it may be worth having a camera on as various elements of non-verbal communication may not translate well if you only use audio.

NOTE

1   At the time of writing (mid-2023), Twitter had not announced its rebranding as X, which occurred in July 2023. I will continue to reference the site by its original name due to this being a recent change and many readers will be more familiar with the original name.

Job Searching 5

Let's start looking for some jobs! But where do you start looking? Your first thought might be to look at some generic job-searching websites, and although they can list some games-development jobs, this isn't the ideal way of finding work within the industry. Instead, multiple game specialist websites can help you find game-specific jobs; this section will highlight a few.

5.1 USEFUL JOB SEARCHING WEBSITES

5.1.1 Game Industry Websites

Now, these aren't consumer-focused sites like IGN or GameSpot. These industry-focused websites discuss topics and news related to game development. Sites such as gameindustry.biz (jobs.gamesindustry.biz/jobs), gamedeveloper.com (jobs.gamedeveloper.com), MCV job board (mcvuk. careerwebsite.com), as well as industry bodies like IGDA and TIGA all have dedicated job pages which can be a good place to start.

5.1.2 gamesjobsdirect.com

This is an online job board (think Indeed.com but for games). The site has a large international database of studios, from small independent companies to large AAA companies. Like with any good job board, you will have various filters to help you find a suitable job. For example, you can search for part-time, remote work. You can also search via your post/zip code to see what is available in your vicinity if you are looking to commute.

DOI: 10.1201/9781003314806-5

5.1.3 gamesjobs.live

Like gamesjobsdirect.com, this is a job board to search for work. However, this site is mainly focused on the UK side of the game industry. Aside from jobs, they also hold online events for all to watch. These can be talks from people within the industry to talk about different topics, give advice, and a career showcase to highlight places to work.

5.1.4 LinkedIn

LinkedIn is one of the world's largest professional networking sites that lets you connect with various professionals in many industries, including games. People will list their educational achievements, career backgrounds such as current and previous roles, and any volunteer experience. There are a large number of game companies that have LinkedIn pages. Many of them share positive articles and social media posts about their company and promote what jobs they offer. Many recruiters and talent scouts will use LinkedIn to search for people who could fit a role they need. Once you gain more experience, you may find that recruiters will start reaching out more. I would advise updating your LinkedIn page as much as possible, adding all the relevant technical and soft skills, educational backgrounds, and work experience to your profile. Think of it as your online CV.

LinkedIn is mainly used professionally; although some people will use safe-for-work jokes and memes to help engage a community, most people will use platforms like Facebook or Twitter to have open discussions about topics brewing within the industry.

5.1.5 workwithindies.com

Maybe you're not interested in going down the AAA route. Perhaps you like working in a smaller team. This site is ideal for those wanting to go down the independent route. Many indie game studios need people to fill particular roles. So indie companies will pay to post job listings on the site for various positions. Of course, not all indies will use this site; some may use their website to promote jobs, but this is a good starting point.

5.1.6 remotegamejobs.com

Since 2020 remote work has become more popular. Many thought working from home in the games industry would be impossible unless you were an indie working on your first project. This site provides a list of jobs for all different skillsets and job titles that can be done remotely.

The year 2020 was challenging for the whole world. Our societal norms pretty much changed overnight. Jobs that were initially considered impossible to do from home became remote (for those sectors that could), and this became the norm for a few years. The games industry had to put a lot of trust in its workers to work from home without breaking their NDA, and many people proved that they could do the job remotely and that maybe this should be an option moving forward rather than limiting options to your workforce. Although some resist the urge to change, it has opened the door for a better work-life balance for people.

5.1.7 hitmarker.net

Hitmarker was launched in 2017 and is an online games job board. Not only does it list development jobs available around the world, but it also lists industry-adjacent roles such as content production and esports roles. Their site also provides gaming news, such as the latest releases. They have a career advice section offering various editorials on getting a job within the industry.

5.1.8 gracklehq.com

Grackle HQ was launched in 2019, and it was created to solve the issue of searching for jobs in different companies and on different job boards. Grackle is a collection of active jobs within the industry to make it easier for people to find work. You don't apply through Grackle; the site only lists minimal details such as job title, company, and location. Each job listing is a hyperlink to the original job posting for you to read up on the details and apply.

5.2 HOW TO FIND GAME COMPANIES

Sometimes not all jobs are advertised on websites like gamesjobsdirect.com, so you might think it is worth looking directly at a game company's website. Rather than trying to remember a huge list of companies, an easier way to find them is by using interactive map sites that collate them in one place to see what companies are available worldwide. These interactive maps can be a helpful tool for anyone looking to relocate or assist with finding studios within your vicinity.

5.2.1 gamedevmap.com

This site lists a large number of game companies located around the world. You can search by city or country to help you get a list of game companies that are registered there. Although it is updated regularly, there is a slight downside. From my personal experience, I have found that sometimes not all the companies listed are active, and there can be quite a few dead links.

5.2.2 gamesmap.uk

If you are in the UK, another useful site to find games companies is gamesmap. uk. This can be helpful to find not just developers and publishers but also can aid in finding available universities and service companies that assist in the development process. This site is more trustworthy as it was built with Ukie and Nesta.

5.2.3 gamesjobs.live

Gamesjobs.live also has an interactive map highlighting companies you can apply for. Again, this one is more UK-focused, but like with gamesmap.uk this one has an air of reliability as the site works with different companies around the UK and is also a member of Ukie.

5.2.4 gamecompanies.com

Lastly we have gamecompanies.com. This site provides information on companies related to the game industry such as developers, publishers, and services companies, as well as the game they have developed over the years. You can use the industries tab to get a list of companies which breaks them down by different continents, counties, and cities to help you see how many companies are available in different areas around the world. Like with the pervious section, there is also an interactive map for you to check out.

5.3 TALENT ACQUISITION

Talent acquisition usually falls under the HR department. Many large game companies will have this dedicated team of people whose task is to find the right person for a job. I spoke with Lukas Genever, senior manager of global talent acquisition at Cloud Imperium Games (CIG), and he described the role as such:

Talent attraction, finding the right people to join CIG, can be anything from headhunting and reviewing CVs. I call it talent branding like the marketing side of CIG to get our word out there, attending events and basically get as much visibility that we can on the roles that we have available.

Quote from Lukas Genever

Talent acquisition will work alongside other departments that are actively recruiting. They can help filter applications for the managers by doing initial passes on applications to see if a person is a right fit for a role. They then give their suggestions to managers to discuss who they want to take forward for interviews.

Because this role entails a lot of outreach work and headhunting, it's worth reaching out to these people to learn more about a company and what you can offer. You can try to contact talent staff on professional websites like LinkedIn; however, depending on the profile of the company they work at, they could get hundreds of messages, so don't expect to get a reply straight away, if at all in some cases. If you want to speak to talent acquisition staff in person, the best places to visit are conference-based games events.

More conference based, our primary target market is gaming professionals, in terms of industry professionals rather than the con-sumer side.

Quote from Lukas Genever

5.4 RECRUITMENT AGENCIES

Recruitment agencies are external companies that help employers find suitable candidates to fill their roles. Agencies will have teams of recruiters actively promoting jobs for their clients (game companies) and supporting their candidates (you).

Going through a recruitment agency can offer benefits such as advice on your application, coaching before interviews, and even providing constructive feedback after an interview. Recruiters are there to help find you the best job that fits your profile and can even help negotiate salaries for roles with a salary range. Just like with job searching, going to any old recruitment agency isn't going to get you anywhere. Instead, you will want to use specialist agencies that deal with the game industry. With video game agencies, the team of recruiters will have a specialism they are assigned to, such as art roles, design, and some will focus primarily on production and QA roles. Table 5.1 lists some game-specific recruiters that you can check out and even contact.

5.5 RELOCATION CONSIDERATIONS

Location is something that you will need to consider when searching for jobs. Each country will have it's hotspots with a large presence of the game

TABLE 5.1 Recruitment agencies

RECRUITERS	DESCRIPTION	WEBSITE
Amiqus	Started in 2000, Amquis is a video game recruiter based in the UK with clients and candidates around the globe.	www.amiqus.com/
Aardvark Swift	Based in Rotherham, Aardvark has been around for over 30 years (1989). They recruit for jobs around the world. They also specialise in graduate and junior recruiting. In fact, Aardvark founded Grads in Games.	aswift.com/
One Player Mission (OPM)	Based in Colchester, UK, OPM has been a games recruiter since 1998. They have worked with over 1,000 companies.	opmjobs.com/
GameLogic	Video game recruiter for studios based in the USA.	www.gamelogicrecruitment. com/

development community and "dead zones" with little to no game development opportunities. Take the UK for example, in the north and south of England, there are many game companies that one can join. However, when you start looking towards the midlands, there might be some smaller indie teams, but larger AA or AAA companies might be more spread out. So you need to think seriously about whether you will commute to work every day, and if so then how, by car or by public transport? Every country will have their hubs for game development, Amanda Lange and Jack Mamais discussed with me the areas in the USA that have the most active development scenes.

> *West coast, it's California, Washington state, there's a bit of a hub in Austin, Texas. Everything's moving to Canada; Montreal gives you the hugest tax reimbursement for moving. Philadelphia has a big indie scene, but even our best indies move to Canada.*
>
> *Quote from Amanda Lange*

> *There's a lot of stuff in Austin, and there's a lot of stuff in Maryland, Bethesda's in Maryland, a lot of work going on up there, and a lot of stuff in Canada. Southeast has a sprinkling of game companies down here, but not heavy; Florida's not that heavy. The West definitely, LA especially, it's pretty heavy, and there's a lot there. But I would say LA and Austin are the two central areas.*
>
> *Quote from Jack Mamais*

Many game companies are located around large cities and metropolitan areas, so if you don't live within a commutable distance, do you want to relocate to another town? If so, is the job you are going for paying a liveable wage, as the cost of living in certain areas can be higher or lower depending on your region.

Maybe the idea of relocating excites you. Perhaps you want to experience a different city or even consider moving to another country for work. The games industry is global, with many roles available worldwide. However, I will have to be the bearer of bad news and say that if you are looking to work abroad as a QA tester, that is extremely unlikely. Getting a work visa is complicated and takes anywhere from 3 months to half a year. Because QA tester is at the base of the hierarchy, these can be seen as more entry-level or junior roles. As such, companies will focus more on recruiting someone closer to the company. If you are applying for leadership jobs like director abroad,

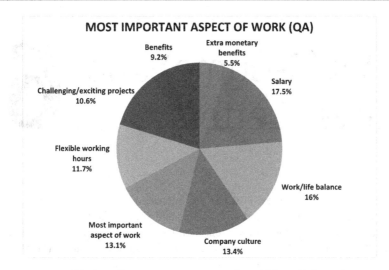

MOST IMPORTANT ASPECT OF WORK (QA)

Benefits
9.2%

Extra monetary
benefits
5.5%

Salary
17.5%

Challenging/exciting projects
10.6%

Flexible working
hours
11.7%

Work/life balance
16%

Most important
aspect of work
13.1%

Company culture
13.4%

FIGURE 5.1 QA data "Most important aspect of work" from Skillsearch.

you will have a better chance of getting interviews. But that will only happen once you get to a level of experience.

Remote and hybrid working is becoming more viable options within the industry, but these options may not be as readily available for QA testers. These might be available for leadership/management positions. Still, the average QA tester probably won't have this option unless it's with a company that works mainly remotely, like indies or smaller- to medium-size AA companies with more remote and hybrid options. Still, I am hopeful that flexible working will become more of a norm. As mentioned earlier, all of our lives have been altered since the 2020 pandemic, people want more flexibility and this is becoming more of a norm in our society. Skillsearch QA data show a combined 27.7% of responses relating to work–life balance and flexible hours as important aspects of work (see Figure 5.1 about other important work aspects responses from QA). Also, in the same QA data, around 90% of QAs are expecting to work remotely at least 1 or more days per week in 2023.

CVs (Resume) and Cover Letters

6

Hopefully, you found a few jobs you are interested in applying for. Well, it's time to dust-off your CV and cover letter and start updating them to show employers why they should hire you. Don't worry if you are unsure how to start; this section will help you design your CV and cover letter for a game-testing job.

6.1 CVS

You want to make sure that your details are available at the top of the page, such as name and number, you can add your address, but that would be optional. You can also provide links to an online portfolio as well. This is obvious, but use a sensible email address, as it will appear unprofessional to future employers. So, try not to use your old anime role-play email address or display name because when you realise you did, you might just end up dying from the cringe.

Provide a list of skills; this can be both technical and soft skills. If you have competent knowledge of particular game engines, software, or even methodologies such as project management (e.g. agile), ensure these are noted. Some people try to make their skills section stand out by using graphs or skill bars (see an example in Figure 6.1). These might make it look visually exciting but ultimately pointless as it will make employers ask more questions. They will consider the criteria and what tests you have used to measure your skill level. Plus, when it comes to ranking ourselves using scales, we can be some-what unreliable and subjective as some may over analyse their skills and rate themselves lower, while others may be a bit more misrepresentative and rate themselves higher. A better alternative would be writing the suitable skill level using words such as "basic", "intermediate", "expert", and "experienced" to

DOI: 10.1201/9781003314806-6

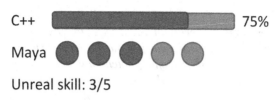

C++   75%

Maya

Unreal skill: 3/5

FIGURE 6.1   Examples of skills scoring.

describe your skill knowledge appropriately. Be as honest as possible with your skill level. It will be pretty easy for an employer to see through your lie during the interview as employers may ask you to demonstrate your skills via a skills test or question you about your knowledge.

Make sure you split your CV into clear sections such as education, skills, and work experience. When listing experience, most people will focus primarily on paid work, but any volunteer work you have done is also valid. Don't worry if your past experiences aren't in the game industry. The months or years of experience in other sectors will be packed with many transferable skills applicable in the industry, and many recruiters will look favourably at those.

> *One of the things I do often look for is retail experience. Because when you work retail, you have to know how to talk to people who aren't necessarily trying to be nice to you, how to diffuse a situation.*
>
> *Quote from Darren Eggerton*

When listing out experiences, try to add details about your roles and responsibilities, especially if they showcase you applying skills that employees are looking for. Some people might not see the direct correlation between a non-industry job and an industry role immediately, so it's important to highlight those links in CVs, cover letters, or even during an interview. If you get stuck about what to include, try looking through the job application again, but this time highlighting any keywords, phrases, or skills employers are seeking. If you have what they are looking for, highlight them in your CV, try adding those keywords and phrases into your application to highlight them where appropriate, such as your work experience.

If you have gaps in your work history, it's best not to try to hide this. Some people might put just the duration of work to hide any gaps, but this will only create more suspicion. I asked Lukas Genever about what talent acquisition look out for in CVs and cover letters, and we discussed gaps in CVs and how you should handle these:

> *Most hiring managers I work with would prefer the years, purely because they have to work backwards if you just put the duration for each of them (jobs). I do understand the benefit of potentially doing the duration, but then it raises more questions rather than answering more.*
>
> *Quote from Lukas Genever*

Ensure you put the years that you have worked and don't worry too much about any noticeable gaps in your work history. Sometimes people have gaps due to personal reasons such as health or economic issues within cities or countries, which means the job market might be dry. Maybe you just took a year or two out to travel the world. You can explain this in your application process; again, trying to be as honest as possible is important.

> *People want to know a reason why someone wasn't working. If it was "they just sat around, did nothing", then you can imagine that wouldn't be that attractive (to an employer). However, if there are other reasons, they're working on a portfolio, they're developing their skills or their getting certifications, that can explain gaps.*
>
> *Quote from Lukas Genever*

6.2 COVER LETTER

You may also be asked to supply a cover letter alongside your CV and job application. Cover letters aren't usually compulsory when applying for a job, but providing one is advised. It allows employers to learn more about you and your personality and offers a good opportunity to showcase why you should be considered for the role.

Recruiters will go through large amounts of applications, so a cover letter can be used to screen applicants who might be similar. A well-crafted and tailored cover letter can improve your chances of standing out in an increasingly competitive market. It's all about selling yourself to an employer. For instance, maybe you just slightly miss some of the qualifications or requirements for a role. If your cover letter can demonstrate your passion, skills, and effort, it could be enough for them to give you a chance for an interview.

Tailoring your letter to the company and role you are applying for is essential. Managers or recruiters don't want to see a generic cover letter that could be sent anywhere. So, the first and most painstakingly obvious thing is to make sure you put the correct company name. People have made this mistake before. I remember a story someone told me of a person applying to TT Games, getting to the interview process, and talking about their love for narrative games as that person had mistaken them for Telltale, so yeah, make sure you know who you are applying to.

This brings me nicely to my next point: research the company you are applying for and use that knowledge in your letter. Learn about the company's history and the games they produce, and use that knowledge to write about why you want to work for them. You might not be able to use all the research in the cover letter, but that knowledge can be helpful during your interview process.

You want to emphasise any skills that will benefit the company or department that you are applying for. Think about what soft and technical skills would be desirable for the job you are applying for. Try looking at the job application and pick out the skills, keywords, and phrases that apply to you and your past experiences. As mentioned in the CVs section, use the job description as a guideline.

> *In your cover letter, highlight why you'd want to work in QA. What experience you do have that you feel has transferable skills, use the job description as a point of reference because if you can highlight, you tick off 1, 2, 3 of the bullet points that are on their (application) because you've done X, Y, Z, then that can highlight why you're a good candidate.*
>
> *Quote from Lukas Genever*

Drawing on previous experiences and how they relate to the job you're applying for can be beneficial. But if you don't have any prior work experience, then this is where you can start to discuss your passion for game development. For instance, if you've done multiple indie projects in your spare time, attended game jams, internships, or even playtesting. All that experience can be related to the job you are applying for.

You could even write about standout moments and achievements to help sell why you should be a part of the team. For example, an old student came to me once for help writing a cover letter. The student told me about a moment during they/them university course when they/them found a unique bug in a programming module. The previous students never encountered this bug. So I said that they/them should add this moment to the cover letter because it shows that they/them was able to think outside the box to find issues, but not only that, they/them was able to fix the issue with little to no support.

You might want to avoid using generic sentences, everyone getting into games is a fan of the media in some way, so it isn't worth mentioning. If you say you're interested in a particular role, then you need to prove it. If you were going for an art job and didn't bother bringing a portfolio, it doesn't show you're serious. For a QA cover letter, talk about bugs you have found in games, any QA research you have done, or even your own QA documentation you have made for a project. You might not be able to add all this to your cover letter, but maybe add it as supplementary material they can refer to.

You don't want to come off cocky or arrogant in your letter as nobody wants to work with someone with a huge ego and it can be damaging to you as well. Finally, avoid repetition; a cover letter is usually of one-page maximum length, so you must get to your point as quickly as possible.

6.3 REJECTION ADVICE

Try not to be demotivated by rejections. It can be difficult to get an email saying that you have been unsuccessful or, even worse, get no reply. You might apply for 50 places and only get 1 or 2 possible interviews, while the rest could be rejected. One way to learn from your rejected applications is to dis-cover what is missing. It may be worth emailing the HR or the recruitment department about your applications. You could reply to the rejection email from HR/recruiter to ask for feedback, but if you cannot do that, many com-panies will have a contact us page on their websites with emails or a text box to submit a question, which could help you get in touch with someone. Some companies may also list a public phone number to ring if you prefer to speak with someone.

You could ask for feedback and find out if anything is missing from your application. I have done this myself in the past. I once applied for three different jobs over a year or two at a particular games company only to be rejected for all of them. Each rejection email was the same copy/paste tem-plate which made me feel very disheartened and frustrated, as I felt that I had relevant experience to at least get an interview. This is when I called up the company and had a discussion with someone in HR who was nice enough to give me feedback on my application and even recommended applying for some upcoming roles.

Not everyone will be able to give feedback as companies get hundreds, if not thousands, of applications, so expect that you may not get a reply. However, if you do, that's great, and hopefully, you get constructive feedback to help you grow and apply that knowledge when reapplying or for other applications.

It's important to note that if you have your heart set on wanting to work at a particular company, don't reapply immediately after your rejection. You won't have had enough time to significantly improve your skills and experience. Also, try not to apply for multiple roles at the same company. This will put people off as it shows that you don't have a clear path and are just looking for any job.

If you weren't successful the first time, any sooner than 6 months, you probably haven't learned any new skills or picked anything else up, but maybe in six months' time, you might have. Then when you do reapply, highlight those new things that you've done. Applying for lots of different positions? don't just apply for everything.

Quote from Lukas Genever

Interviewing for a QA Job

7

If you successfully get through the first part of the application process, you will get the chance to take part in an interview. This is probably the most nerve-racking part of any job application. So it's pretty natural to be a little nervous about interviews. You're going to be in a room with at least one person (possibly up to two to three people) who you have never met before and who are judging everything from what you say, how you say it, and maybe even how you dress.

Preparing yourself is good, and this section will do just that. Maybe you are reading this on the way to an interview. Hopefully, this chapter will help you nail that interview if that's the case!

Some ways of alleviating the pressure of an interview could be doing mock interviews with friends or even family. This can help you get familiar with the interviewing process, help you prepare, and boost your confidence. By doing mock interviews, you can ask people for feedback, make sure that whoever is giving you feedback provides quality feedback that will help you improve yourself. It's not helpful to anyone if they just say you did well. Make sure people provide you with something of substance.

7.1 SIGNING NDAS

Non-disclosure agreements (NDAs) are critical when you go for interviews and when you get a job at a company, so if you do get an interview, one of the first things you will be asked to sign is an NDA. Essentially, this is a legal document which means that you cannot talk about the inner workings of a company or discuss any unreleased content currently in development. This is to ensure that nothing is leaked before official announcements are made. If you break NDAs, this can lead to your termination as you have violated your contract. This could also have a residual effect on the department. If higher-ups

DOI: 10.1201/9781003314806-7

feel the department cannot be trusted, they could revoke certain rights and privileges. Leaking can also lead to you being blackballed, which means that other companies will refuse to hire you due to your past actions. They know you can't be trusted, so be careful what you say to friends, family, or peers.

7.2 PRESENTING YOURSELF

You'll find that most people's work attire is casual when working in the industry. Wear whatever is comfortable for you. When it comes to interviews, you want to make a good impression. Most of us have had this advice throughout our lives when it comes to interviews: to dress smart. This is to show that you are putting in the effort. When it comes to game industry interviews, most are okay with casual clothing. If you are unsure, you can always contact HR or recruitment, who will tell you the dress code for the interview. But usually, this info is in the email you get when you are offered an interview. I like to try to go with a smart causal look as I think it's a nice blend between formal and informal as it still shows you put in the effort for the interview. It goes without saying that dress sense is not the only thing to think about, but personal hygiene as well. So maybe use that perfume or cologne that you save for nights out or special occasions.

You should try to be conscious of body language during your interview. Make sure your posture is good, so do not slouch in your seat, as it will seem like you are bored and uninterested. Mirror the interviewer's body and facial language to help make sure yours is appropriate for the conversation. Reading the interviewer's body and facial language can also help you gauge how well the interview is going. I understand that if you are neurodiverse, this can be more difficult, and you may use masking more consciously to help pick up social cues.

For a QA role, especially for entry-level ones, a key aspect that interviewers will be looking out for is the interviewee's personality, such as character traits, attitudes, and behaviour. They want to gauge your characteristics to see if they will benefit and grow the team rather than hamper it. QA is a team effort, and it's important that anyone who is brought to the team can work well with others, contribute positively to the work environment, and allow for healthy discussions to grow. Suppose you are aggressive, abrasive, or lacking empathy towards others. In that case, interviewers may pick up on these during the interview or even based on your previous employment record. For example, you were a QA contractor for a long time, looking for a permanent position but unable to secure one. Part of it could be bad luck, missing a specific skill or no permanent work available, but maybe an element of it could be your personality.

> *you can get stuck in that loop where you are, contract after contract, after contract, not securing a permanent position, and when I have applicants like that, I can sometimes see, in the interview, why maybe their contract wasn't extended.*
>
> *You can catch early red flags in an interview. Such as someone that keeps waffling on about a point. If you ask them a direct question, which warrants a one-minute answer, they will just keep going off on a tangent. That's a big red flag because they lack the conciseness and clarity, and maybe confidence in their answer. In QA, where you have to write multiple bug reports a day, being succinct and able to communicate clearly is paramount.*
>
> *Quote from Naveen Yadav*

It's worth noting that you shouldn't be afraid to voice your opinion, concerns, or complaints. A good company should be willing to listen to the concerns of it's workforce. If you can make suggestions or provide alternative solutions to a problem or task, you should be able to voice them professionally. Some of this advice is for when you are in a workplace, but if you are asked to express your opinion about their work, make sure it is civil discussion.

> *Try to show who you are because if you're not gonna fit in the environment, then it's better to know earlier rather than later. You don't want to come off as like a corporate drone just to try and get yourself in there.*
>
> *Quote from Darren Eggerton*

7.3 VIRTUAL INTERVIEWS

Video calls can be used to conduct interviews. Some companies may use it to screen applicants before a full in-depth interview. If you are doing virtual interviews, make sure you have a webcam available on your laptop/PC, a headset would be ideal because those inbuilt mics on webcams are just the worse. You don't need to break the bank for an expensive headset just so long as the quality of the mic is okay and you have some noise suppression in case you have a loud fan or background noise that could be distracting. Even though you are doing an online interview, it is still worth keeping your appearance clean and professional as if you were doing an in-person interview. The same goes for your surroundings as well. Try to find a quiet place where you can interview with little to no distractions, and if interviewers can see the room in the background, like, your home office, it might be worth cleaning the room just to be safe. Finally, double-check your internet connection; try calling someone on Zoom, Teams, or Discord to see if you have a stable enough connection to maintain an hour-long call.

Some interviews may only be one meeting, but some can have multiple interview stages. Naveen, the QA manager from nDreams, discussed how they have an initial phone screening to get to know the interviewee before deciding if they go through to the first interview stage.

> *if they're successful in that phone screening, then they get put into the first interview stage for the QA role; we only limit it to those two. For the more technical roles, we'll open it up to a second stage and then the final stage.*
>
> *Quote from Naveen Yadav*

7.4 RESEARCH THE COMPANY

As mentioned in the Cover Letter section of Chapter 6, you should research the company you plan to work for. If you get to the interviewing stage, the interviewers will most likely ask you why you want to work for them, which games of theirs you like, and even what you know about the company (this could be a brief history or even knowledge of partnerships or how many studios they have). It shows that you've put on in the effort.

Play the company's games (if you have the time and can afford to). This isn't necessarily a must for the interview but can benefit your skills test as it can be based on their recent games, so knowing how to play their games will make it easier to find bugs. If you can't afford or don't have access to systems to play games, it's worth watching playthroughs, looking up guides on the game, or even learning the control scheme online.

When I was given the interview at Cloud Imperium Games (CIG), I bought Star Citizen to play. I followed the game's development a bit, but decided to purchase the game to play in preparation for my interview. The PC I had in 2019 was already 4 years old at this point, so I barely met the requirements to play the game, but I tried and got somewhat familiar with the game before my interview, which helped. It also gave me something to talk about as well. This brings me to my second point: if you have played or have good knowledge of a company's products, interviewers will most likely ask for your opinion and feedback about their game. This is where you can discuss what you like about their game/s and any constructive feedback about their products. The interviewers may even ask you what could be done to improve it. So don't just say, "I didn't like it", or "I thought it was crap" because it has no substance and is quite frankly unprofessional if you're speaking in a derogatory sense about people's hard work. At CIG, I was on the interviewing panel for a second embedded tester to work alongside me. During the interview, panel members would ask the interviewee for their opinions on the game and how things can be improved. If a candidate could give qualitative feedback about the game's features or location with solid reasoning, it showcased their communication skills and demonstrated different critical thinking elements. This also showcases your ability to analyse the situation around you and creatively think of solutions backed up by an understanding of game design principles. Janel Jolly spoke about some of the questions they asked during a QA tester interview.

> *We do like to ask what game you have played. We ask, why do you think that is a high-quality game? What is the worst-quality game you ever played? Why? Because quality is the management of expectations. Always go into the meeting with a game in your pocket that you think is high quality, a game that you think is low quality, and make sure to list a bug from a game you have observed.*
>
> *And if you haven't observed, then at least research it. Be willing to talk about that and never lie in an interview, especially regarding "yes, I played your game before" cause you're gonna get very grilled on their product. And if you can drive that conversation to, "I've only played a bit of your game, but actually, I really like Diablo 3 though. Do you mind if I use that as an example for a bug?" so try and own the conversation towards it.*
>
> *Quote from Janel Jolly*

7.5 GAME TESTING SKILLS TEST

Some QA testing interviews will have skills test. It's not uncommon for many game industry jobs to have some tests to demonstrate that you can do the job. For a QA role, you will most likely be playing either an old build from their back catalogue of games or a purpose-built one specifically for interviews.

These specific builds will be based on their existing games, but have been tweaked slightly so that bugs are present for interviewees to find. Some tests may require you to go through specific instructions in which you will have to mentally note things you have seen along the way, as the interviewer will ask you questions based on them.

Or you will be given an allotted amount of time, usually an hour, to play a game, find bugs, and make bug reports. From my experience, these bug reports have usually been handwritten, so you may want to brush up on your handwriting. However, if you cannot write things down due to pre-existing medical conditions, you may need to stipulate that before the interview so that reasonable adjustments can be made, such as a laptop for you to use.

An hour isn't a lot of time, so try to use it as best as possible. You need to find the fine line between quality and quantity. You may find a lot of bugs, but if your bug reports are incomprehensive and lacklustre, that will mark against you.

Alternatives to tests could be questions asked to you. I remember in the past when getting interviewed for QA tester roles. The interviewers would give me a hypothetical scenario such as "You're playing a new level for game X; how would you test it?" or even something as simple as "How would you test a pen?". This seems simple, but it does help to demonstrate a person's thought process and is another chance to showcase your critical thinking skills. Of course, when asked how to test something, you could start with the obvious answers, but you should try to think outside of the box and think of commonly overlooked tests. If you mention those, you may impress the interviewer.

I've also used example bugs, give them a situation and say, "Here's a bug, you know this piece of knowledge about the situation and what you're gonna do to investigate and try and figure out how to reproduce this bug". And I'm not even using a real-life bug; I'm just making something up and seeing how they kind of probe at it.

I've seen practical tests, like being dumped on a build and asked to find and report bugs, like actual writeups. At one point at team17, when I was hiring, I put together a five-minute video of one of our games. And in these five minutes, there were over 30 bugs visible, and it was kind of just like, "Here's a video; give me everything you can spot". You can watch it a couple of times, write down as much as you can find. If they can give me a list of more than anything that's super obvious, That's a bonus, but again, not essential, just any kind of proof that they are observant.

Quote from Darren Eggerton

> *If it was an entry-level position like at University Speaking, back then (2018), we did have them do a little skills test where I think it was, a snippet of a game, asked them to point out what issues are present in the picture. That was pretty much the skills test there, though it may have changed now.*
>
> *Quote from Naveen Yadav*

7.6 TALKING ABOUT SKILLS

You could be asked during the interview about what skills you have, why those skills are good for that role, or if you have ever found bugs in other games before. When answering these types of questions, you want to highlight the qualities and skills the interviewers are looking for. Understanding QA's role in the game development pipeline is very important due to people's assumptions about what QA is. Discussing problem-solving and critical thinking skills with examples from your life or previous jobs will help show your potential employers why you would fit in with their department. Even just talking about these can demonstrate your conversational skills. Articulating your points showcases your communication skills and how effective they are.

> *We really do look for critical thinking. We look for conversation skills. We look for people who are not yes Men. We also look for people who understand, what a bug is, and that sounds really funny, but too often, people think a bug is a bad design, or they think that being in QA is about feedback. It's not feedback, it's defects and bugs, like an unintended outcome, it's unplanned.*
>
> *Quote from Janel Jolly*

One method that can help with answering questions during an interview is the STAR method. This method effectively structures your answers to highlight your skills and qualities. It's especially helpful when talking about your experiences as it frames around your actions and abilities.

STAR stands for:

- *Situation*: Describing the situation you had to deal with, what happened, when it took place
- *Task*: Your responsibility in the situation, what the goal was
- *Action*: Details on what steps you took to complete the task, how you solved the problem
- *Result*: The outcomes achieved from your actions.

Even if you haven't worked in the industry beforehand, don't be afraid to discuss relevant work experiences or situations when applying the STAR method. Because if you can talk about how you demonstrated your negotiation, communication, and problem-solving skills in real-world scenarios, people can see how those skills you have refined in your previous experiences can transfer into your potential new job. Especially if it's a stressful job like in retail because anyone who can deal with the high-pressure situations that come from working in those kinds of jobs will have many outstanding characteristics ideal in a game development environment.

A lot of times, people leave out that they worked at McDonald's or they worked at fast food or construction. In QA we love hearing that because that's proof that you work someplace, that's high process driven, that's high stress-driven, and you showed up to work. That says a lot about someone's character. So, when you are applying for a job in QA, don't be shy about other jobs that might not be seen as significant because there's so many skills that can be transferred.

Quote from Janel Jolly

7.7 ASK QUESTIONS

At the end of the interview, you are usually asked if you have any questions for the interviewers. This is an excellent opportunity to learn more about the department and the company. Try preparing some questions beforehand. This will show you're interested and enthusiastic about the role. I always like to write down questions I want to ask interviewers a day before on my phone or in a notebook, I try to memorise them, but there's no harm in asking interviewers if you can refer to your notes for questions. I have done that myself, as I usually bring a notebook to note things interviewers bring up during the interview or answers to my questions. Think to yourself, what do you want to learn about the company? Are there any benefits that you want to be aware of? What are their policies for remote work? Interviewers can bring up your main question about pay during the interview or afterwards when they give you the job offer, so don't focus too much on that for now (mainly due to the social stigma we talked about in Chapter 2). Instead, try to learn as much about the company and its culture as possible to see if you feel like this is a place worth staying at and can see yourself working long-term, possibly progressing internally.

7.8 WHERE DO YOU SEE YOURSELF IN 5 YEARS?

This question (or a variation of it) always appears during the interview process. Managers will ask this question to see if the person they are hiring is interested in the role and wants to progress within it. This shows managers that the potential employee is looking to contribute and grow within the company instead of just doing it for a pay check. It also helps to see if your goals align with the companies. If so, they will help you towards them because it may motivate you to be more productive, and you will most likely stay there longer. It also helps to inform employers about that person and if they are looking to stay at the company long term. Hiring and onboarding someone is a costly and lengthy process, so they want to make sure that they are investing in someone who wants to stay for a good amount of time.

The interesting thing about a QA tester role is that it's okay to talk about wanting to grow your career outside the department. People have used game-testing jobs for years to launch their careers in other disciplines. QA managers are aware of that and can support your career ambitions outside of the QA department and may even actively support you. So don't feel afraid to discuss this because, most likely, they are expecting you to say you want to go into a production, art, or design role.

Something that I noticed, which is unique to QA, is we want to know your career ambitions. Because not many people want to build a career in QA. So, when we understand what career you want to do, that always comes with an expectation or assumption that you're using this to bounce towards the job you want. And throughout QA in gaming, that's acceptable, that's expected, and that's encouraged.

Quote from Janel Jolly

Personally, I very much dislike this question because we don't know where we will be in a couple of years' time. Things that were once important to us might not necessarily be as important a month, two months, or even a year from now. This question kind of hurts me because I once tried to plan out a good portion of my life and when I got to my mid 20s, things didn't turn out the way I hoped, this hurt me emotionally and mentally. I had to learn to be more adaptable to go with the flow. Anyone who knows me knows that I can be a bit of a stickler when organising things, but I actively don't try to plan out the next three or five years of my life. I try to keep most of my long-term goals achievable within a year or so. Sometimes, people might not know exactly where they want to be in a few years, and that's okay. Ask yourself questions about what you want to do, where you want to be, and take some time to find your focus and purpose. I recognise that went a little bit deep with a very simple interview question, but it puts some undue pressure on you to have your life figured out when really we're all still trying to figure that out ourselves daily.

Working in QA
Everyday Tips and Skills

8

This section is intended for anyone looking to learn more about the QA process for their job applications. But it can also be helpful for those just starting their first day or week in a brand new QA job! In this section, we will go over some general advice that can be used and some advice if you are looking to progress within the QA department.

8.1 SOFT SKILLS

It's not just technical skills that are important in QA or other jobs in the industry, but soft skills. These skills range from motivation, teamwork, problem-solving, adaptability, positive attitudes, and time management. Think about your strongest soft skills and which ones are your weakest. Understanding yourself is valuable as you can take steps to improve yourself. In QA, you aren't isolated in a bubble; you are part of a team, and not having specific soft skills can be a detriment to the rest of the department.

8.1.1 Communication

Good verbal and written communication is vital within a work environment. It will become more invaluable as you move up the hierarchy as there will be more visibility on you from management, producers, and even executives. You may also become a point of contact for new starters or other QA testers, so articulating your point as efficiently as possible is critical to ensure nothing is lost in translation. This is vital in any role you do, not just QA.

DOI: 10.1201/9781003314806-8

Most of your communication will be through emails and chat software such as Outlook, Microsoft Teams, or Slack. Most of the time, you will use the company's preferred chat system to talk to anyone. Because you will mostly be communicating through text, remember that your tone can be lost or misinterpreted in your messages.

Be proactive in the chats; if you see an issue, call it out so other team members know it. Maybe someone else is already bugging it, so ask if anyone is familiar with the issue or if anyone's also writing it up. You don't want to be in a situation where two people are writing up the same bug due to miscommunication, as this will waste both testers' time.

8.1.2 Interpersonal Skills

This segment does intertwine with your communication skills. Here, we will essentially mix various soft skills, such as leadership, teamwork, etc., as I figured it would be best to put them all under this one heading rather than list them individually. Game development is a collaborative process. You will be working and engaging with other people during a project. Even if you are a solo indie developer, at some point, you will be in discussions with other people (e.g. marketing, publishers), so you must be able to work well and connect with people, whether managers or co-workers.

One skill that will be useful is active listening. This does exactly what is said on the tin; you are fully concentrating on what is being said rather than just passively "hearing" the speaker's message. This can be shown through verbal and non-verbal communication, such as your posture, eye contact, questioning, and clarification, to name a few.

Emotional intelligence is key when developing communication, teamwork, and leadership skills. This is best described as recognising and managing your emotions and the emotions around you. Understanding these emotions and how you respond to them can positively or negatively impact your workplace. Working on your emotional intelligence will help you better handle conflicts and stress in the workplace and build better relationships with your team.

Maybe you feel like you need to work on your emotional intelligence. In that case, there are many great articles online that can help (my personal favourite being Roch Maritin's article: "50 Tips for Improving Your Emotional Intelligence"[1]). You can improve your emotional intelligence by being more self-aware and reflecting on your thoughts and emotions, how they impact you, and how you interact with others. Try to be more empathic and understand other people's perspectives and feelings. Work on managing your stresses by practising mindfulness and breathing techniques.

If you are neurodiverse, some elements of communication and interpersonal skills might be more challenging to read, such as expressions, body language, or even social cues and nuances (e.g. sarcasm or ambiguous statements). Many neurodiverse people can use "masking" to hide parts of themselves to "fit in" around others. Masking is something everyone unconsciously does. However, someone who is neurodivergent may use masking more to mimic behaviours and social scripting to blend in with others. This adds pressure as trying to "fit in" can harm your mental health as you are using a lot of your energy on supressing elements of yourself and your own identity, which can lead to burnout, leading to anxiety and depression. Practising more self-care and being more self-conscious of how you are using masking can help towards better kindness and compassion within yourself to reduce internal stigmas and change negative views on masking. Overall better public awareness and knowledge about neurodiverse behaviours can help reduce stigma and judgement. Although these large shifts in societal thinking can take a long time to become integrated into society, these are small steps to help make those changes.

I am not an expert in neurodiversity. This section was written based on my knowledge, experiences, and research. I would encourage people to learn more about neurodiversity to better understand people's conditions, difficulties, and ways that you can be more understanding and make reasonable adjustments when needed. (There is an excellent GDC talk that I recommend watching: *What Being Neurodivergent Means in Game Development.*[2])

8.1.3 Problem-Solving

This is a vital part of the testing process; you may find yourself testing a new mechanic or location only to encounter bugs such as an exploit, the game crashing, or a game mechanic just no longer working. This is where your problem-solving skills will come into play. You need to retrace your steps and think about what you have done, and sometimes it can be pretty difficult to reproduce a bug, so you have to think of all the different variables that could have resulted in causing the issue to occur.

The first thing that you want to do is understand what the problem is. If you know what the problem is, you can better describe what needs to be fixed. You also want to find the root cause of the issue; you can identify the symptoms of the problems, but can you show and explain what causes the issue?

8.1.4 Time Management

Developing these skills will help you be more employable. If you lack time management, employers may find you to be more of a liability than an asset.

Improving these skills will help you be a better tester and can be beneficial if you wish to progress within the department.

There are ways you can improve and develop this skill, such as focusing on one task at a time. Multitasking may sound like you are getting more done, but it can cause you to split your focus, so doing one task at a time can help you produce better work and will help you feel less overwhelmed.

You can break down larger tasks into smaller, more manageable goals that you can complete to help you get to your final objective. Set deadlines for tasks and try to stick to these. There are various time management tools that you can use (either digital or physical) such as desk dairy, calendars, or even note and time-tracking software.

Take breaks to give yourself some time to refresh. This can help you refocus; maybe you will have that eureka moment while making a cup of tea. Working non-stop is unhealthy, so take it easy on yourself; otherwise, you'll burn out.

8.2 EVERYDAY TASKS YOU CAN DO

If you start work earlier than your leads, you may not have any tasks to jump onto. So when you find yourself in this position, it's good to be proactive and think of tasks you can do before moving on to your official tasks.

The first go-to activity you can do is to check if any bugs have been NMI'd. Sometimes bugs can be sent back to you as "needs more info (NMI)", this could be due to developers needing extra information such as "Does this happen at X level" or "Does this affect X". This can be helpful to them to see if an issue is just local to a specific area or a specific mechanic. They could need additional data using console variables (CVARs) for extra debugging data. The information on the report might not be clear or missing required files such as screenshots or videos, so you may need to rectify any errors.

Other tasks that can do are retesting any resolved issues. There may be a filter that the QA team uses to retest any high-priority issues to ensure they are fixed, or you can retest any resolved or open issues that you have reported to confirm they are still present or if not, then you can close off the issue. You could also use this time for self-development; if QA provides any documentation, it would be worth reviewing them to understand the department and its procedures better.

8.3 NEVER ASSUME!

When you are testing a game, and you come across an issue that you are unsure if it's a feature or a bug, make sure to investigate it and get confirmation. You can do this by asking people or looking at any documentation about the game, such as design documents. One piece of advice I remember from my first industry job was "never assume"; this was written on the whiteboard in the QA department. If you leave a potential issue thinking it's not a bug, maybe the next tester will think the same and the next, which might then cause everyone to make the same assumptions until someone calls it out, saying "Why hasn't this been bug?", so always do your due diligence. Confirm if something is or isn't an issue, even if you don't have the time to investigate. Note it for something to look into tomorrow or call it out in your QA chats; maybe one of your teammates has some time to help.

8.4 THINKING OUTSIDE THE BOX

When testing, it can be at first daunting because you have so many systems and features to investigate you might not know where to start. The first thing can be reviewing the most noticeable and commonly used areas and components to ensure there are no significant blocker issues that halt the players' progression and that a system's basic functions are working as intended (e.g. a weapon can be reloaded, fired, etc.). Next, experiment with the game to find issues that might not be as obvious. A good question you can ask yourself while testing is, "What happens if I do…?". It's a simple phrase but a good starting point to help you think outside the box and open up alternatives. Here is an example "Oh, I was able to go through that door fine, but what happens if 2 people go through it at the same time? What happens if I run into the door? What happens if I try to fit a car or bike through it?". Bit of a simple example but hopefully you can see how this can help you start experimenting with alternative test cases.

Another way to help you find issues is by using the scientific method. You probably have learnt this method in school and will recognise the cycle given in Figure 8.1. So why am I telling you about this? It's because there are quite a few parallels between testing and gathering scientific data. The scientific method is all about gathering empirical evidence, which means information gather through observation and experimentation to prove or disprove a hypothesis. Let's have a brief look at each of these steps, and

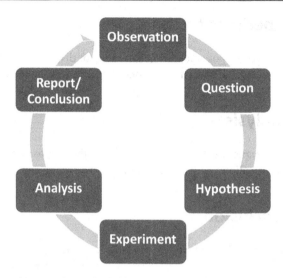

FIGURE 8.1 The scientific method diagram.

hopefully, you can see how the scientific method can be incorporated into testing:

8.4.1 Observation

The first step is to observe the software, so to do this you need to play it, learn the product, and observe how it behaves (functions systems, game flow).

8.4.2 Question

As you observe, ask yourself questions about what can be tested and how it can be tested (you could use the "what happens if I do X?" question as discussed earlier).

8.4.3 Hypothesis

Maybe you see a bug and have an assumption as to the cause. Here you can make an educated guess about the cause of the issue and create your hypothesis on why it occurred or how to make it happen again. Here you can start making predictions on what you think will happen if you do X or Y in an attempt to break a system or feature based on your observations.

8.4.4 Experiment

Execute tests to reveal potential failures to prove or disprove your hypothesis, and collect any valuable data (if any) from your tests (e.g. debug info).

8.4.5 Analysis

After you have experimented a few times to get the bug to happen, you can analyse the information you gathered and explain how you caused the issue.

8.4.6 Conclusion

Based on the analysis, you should be able to articulately write a report explaining the issue and how to reproduce it, with supplementary data such as screenshots and videos with any relevant debugging information needed.

8.5 GENERAL QA ADVICE

8.5.1 Taking on Extra Responsibilities

If you intend to work up the ladder, make sure you are getting noticed. People can overlook you if you stay quiet and just do the job, so it would be wise to have a good working relationship with the other testers, seniors, leads, and management. One of the ways that you could do this is by being proactive during the day's tasks, for example actively communicating in team chats. If any email updates need to go out to the QA team or other departments, volunteer to complete this task. The same can be said for any handover comments as well. If people know you're the go-to person to provide information, it will show that you're looking for more responsibility; as such, QA leadership will know they can rely on you for support. This can help make you a prime candidate for a possible senior role.

8.5.2 Repetition

The repetitive nature of a QA job is something to be aware of. Video game development, especially in the AAA market, can take years before it's publicly available. So as much as your nephew might think it's cool that you play games for a living, don't forget you're testing the same game for 8 hours a day for potentially 4-5 years. So, you might find there will be times when motivation will start to decrease. Try to find a way to keep yourself motivated and energised. Try to find new challenges in your work, and keep experimenting as much as possible to keep testing interesting. Ask if other tasks can be worked on to avoid getting stuck in a routine. If there is a possibility to upskill yourself in the QA department, take that opportunity. Maybe you can develop a specialism within the department that can be beneficial. Suppose you end up in a senior or leadership position. In that case, it's essential to keep the team energised and enthused, so team outings, game tournaments, or playtesting sessions might provide a breath of fresh air for everyone.

8.5.3 Sticky Notes, Emails, and Bookmarks

Sticky notes are your best friend; use them wherever appropriate, as they can be a time saver. For me, they have many uses, for example listing essential details for the day, such as listing build numbers, as this will save time when entering build IDs on new bug reports or providing build IDs to people who ask for it. I would also advise listing all your most commonly used CVARs on a sticky note rather than going to a web page or document. Having them on a note can let you have them nearby on a separate screen to refer back to quickly. Another valuable use of sticky notes is to have bug report templates. You will find that many of your Jira's will start the same, so rather than having to type these out each time, having a base to start will save you a lot of time.

Like with many office jobs, you will eventually get swamped with a ton of emails. As such, it's best to organise your email inbox. First, create folders to manage all the different types of emails. This is a must, as you will get many emails from monthly reports, sanity checks, flare threads, and automated emails created by automated testing systems. If you don't organise these correctly, you will miss critical updates. Many email applications, such as Outlook, will allow users to create rules that automatically sort emails into folders based on your set rules.

If your company has online project management software such as Confluence, Jira, or their equivalents, make sure to have these bookmarked. I would have various bookmark folders on different topics from general admin (HR-related sites), embedded documentation, useful QA bugging pages. For a hugely complex game like Star Citizen, there were many procedures on how to bug specific systems and features, and memorising all this information can be tricky, so having them easily accessible via bookmarks helped make sure that I had quick access to the most common pages I needed.

8.6 SOFTWARE

Aside from needing to master the game, you will also need to master the various software used by the company you are working for (e.g. issue trackers, version control, and project management). These are used to add, update, and track tasks and bugs in an extensive database for people in the company. Various departments use this database of issues and tasks to collect data for reports on the progress of a game feature and even listing major issues halting development. There are various tracking and management software on the market. Many companies will use several industry-standard software, so let's outline some of these here.

8.6.1 Jira and Confluence

Jira is an issue-tracking software developed by Atlassian. It is designed to report and track issues but has evolved to be a useful management tool. Users can create Kaban boards to visually track the progress of tasks and create dashboards to act as a hub for your team or department. For instance, you can create a dashboard for the QA department to keep track of the bugs, such as a table of major critical and blocker issues and a pie chart that visually shows the total number of bugs and how many are open or closed. If you are a producer, you could create a dashboard for your specific team to use as a hub to track tasks and issues related to that team. Many game companies use Jira, as it's an industry-standard software.

Confluence is another Atlassian product. It's a wiki software that allows teams to create workspaces to house pages for your needs. You can use it to create training or how-to-guide documentation on internal tools. Confluence can also be used to develop game design documentation, for example breaking down a level flow, and detailing game mechanics or characters. From a QA point of view, why would you ever need to use this? QA can create pages dedicated to teaching people how to write up bugs according to their internal procedures. They may have pages on how to bug AI or mission content, as there could be conditions and CVARs needed for a bug report so that the teams handling these features have the information required to fix the issue. Access to the broader game development documentation will help you better understand the game and help you be a better tester. Maybe you want to learn more about a location or mission in the game. Having pages on these subjects will give you that insight and answer any questions you may have about the game's content.

8.6.2 Bugzilla

This is a web-based open-source defect-tracking system. Its primary function is creating and tracking issues, and various organisations have used it. Because Bugzilla is open source, users have more options to customise it as they see fit. One of the unique selling points Bugzilla boasts is that they have many features that their paid counterparts lack. And to top it off, it's completely free, so large companies do not just use it, but smaller teams and even solo developers.

8.6.3 Perforce: Helix Visual Client

Perforce is a company that specialises in development and DevOps software for various industries, such as management tools to version control software. The game industry uses various pieces of Perforce software, especially the Helix Visual Client (also known as P4V), version control software. Many industry-standard software, such as Unreal Engine, Unity, and 3DS Max, can connect directly to P4V to download files from the server. That way, you have them locally and upload these files back to the server (if they have been checked out of P4V for editing).

From a general QA standpoint, this might not be something you will use but more technical roles and embedded positions may use this software more frequently. For example, developers may want their work checked in the game by QA to ensure no major bugs. You may pull files from the server to get them locally to check for issues. If you are in an embedded position, you may be able to provide some development support, such as bug fixing or smaller development tasks.

8.6.4 Hansoft

Another piece of Perforce software. This tool is used for project planning as it allows users to plan and track projects and fit them within their chosen project management method, such as waterfall or agile. Users can create dashboards, track time, and use Kaban boards, similar to Jira. One of the features Hansoft has is issue-tracking features, so you can create bug reports and track them.

8.6.5 TestRail

This web-based test case management software is used extensively in QA for both the games and software industries as it allows users to design test cases, design and run test suites, and track the results. The benefit of using TestRail is that it will enable users to get real-time updates on the progress of the test suite. In addition, users will get a pie chart with statistics breaking down the results of test cases. This can be great information to pass on to leadership if they require progress updates and can be used for production meetings to see the state of mechanics, areas, etc., that have been tested. TestRail also integrates with Jira, meaning any bugs, tasks, etc., linked to a test case on TestRail will have Jira hyperlinks.

8.6.6 Excel

Maybe you haven't needed this classic spreadsheet software much since school, but it might be worth brushing up on how to use it. Excel is frequently used by QA and other departments, such as production, as it can be a convenient tool for creating budget plans and creating and maintaining schedules. QA can also use it to create test suites and issue-tracking documents. These documents will be available online (such as SharePoint), so multiple QA team members can work on the same document, allowing viewers to update results in real time.

It's worth researching formulas that could help update Excel test sheets, such as formulas that allow you to add bug ID number, which then links to the bug report webpage, drop-down lists, and even calculating time (this will be especially useful for multiplayer games if you want to calculate the time how long a tester has been in a server).

8.6.7 Software: General Advice

If you haven't used the software listed earlier, I would highly advise you to check out if they have a free trial or if you can create an account to access a free version. Many project management software allows users a free version, but many advanced features will be locked away behind a paywall. If that's the case, still use the free version to learn the fundamentals of the software. That way, you can learn how to set up your bug reports, such as what fields people need to fill in, the workflow for reports, and custom fields people need to fill in.

Take for instance Atlassian, you can create an account and a project on various software such as Jira and Confluence. You can also have up to 10 users on your Atlassian sites (Jira dashboard or wiki pages), if you are working on a team game for a games jam, education, or doing a side project. You can utilise these sites to help manage yourself. However, it also gives you a chance to build your skills in this software which can be an excellent benefit for you during the application stage or even when you start your QA job, as you will have an advantage over those who have never used them.

NOTES

1 "50 Tips for Improving Your Emotional Intelligence". Published on January 12, 2022. Available at: https://www.rochemartin.com/blog/50-tips-improving-emotional-intelligence

2 Available at: https://www.gdcvault.com/play/1027729/What-Being-Neurodivergent-Means-in

Bug Report Breakdown

9

Here we will break down different elements of a bug report that you as a tester will fill in. One thing to remember is that each company will have their own bug templates, which could be arranged differently than another company, or they could have extra or fewer elements. So this chapter will be a good starting point for understanding the structure of a bug report.

9.1 SUMMARY

The definition of a summary is a brief statement of the main points of something (in this case, the main points of your bug). You can look at your summary as the title of your bug report. When other testers search for issues in the database, such as Jira, this is the first thing they will see. Each company will have a standardised way of summarising a bug. Below are some formatting examples to help you understand what a summary could look like.

- *Game – mode (if applicable) – level – specific location – component/feature type – device/systems (if applicable) – brief description*
- *Level – device/systems (if applicable) – specific location – component/feature type – brief description*

It's important when writing a summary to provide the necessary information quickly and concisely in the report summary to make it easier for any developer, QA tester, or producer who is searching for existing reports. Before putting a bug in, search the issue tracker database for any similar issues. It's important to remember that (excluding automated tests and crashes) all the tasks and issues in the database are written up by human beings. So, everyone will have their own way of summarising an issue. For example, if you see a hole in a wall, one person could write in their summary, "There is a hole

 DOI: 10.1201/9781003314806-9

in the wall at location X", in contrast, another person could write, "There is missing geometry on the wall at location X". Both are equally valid summaries and explain the issue. Still, when searching the issue in Jira, you can easily miss a bug if you don't search for the correct wording. One issue could be summarised in various ways, so it's important to think of keywords or phrases most likely to be searched.

Don't make your summary too wordy. It shouldn't be bogged down by giving the exact specifics. That kind of information can be provided in the description of your bug. It's like when you write the subject of an email; you don't give a long-winded explanation; it's short and provides an idea of what that email is at first glance.

9.2 PRIORITY AND SEVERITY

When you report an issue, you need to think about how severe the problem is, how badly it impacts gameplay, does it prevent players from progressing, and whether there are noticeable issues that players can see. This is where you would input the priority and severity of the issue to help inform producers and development teams about how urgent the issue is and which problems need fixing first.

Both might seem similar, but an easy way to remember the difference between them is the severity is how much impact the issue has on the end-user experience. In contrast, priority measures the issue's urgency and how quickly it needs fixing.

Not all companies will use severity and priority; some could primarily use priority or vice versa. Table 9.1 gives an example of severity levels and priority levels. Remember that each company will have their own naming conventions for priorities and different severity levels, but principles are still the same.

9.3 COMPONENTS

This is where you will list all the components related to your issue. Each game element will have its own label in the component section. Components are vital as they allow for better organisation, and filtering issues via their components will be much easier. If you had a bug where weapon sound effects were missing, or dialogue was corrupted, you would add components such as SFX audio and dialogue for those respective issues. Companies will have

TABLE 9.1   Severity and priority level description

SEVERITY LEVELS	PRIORITY LEVELS	DESCRIPTION	EXAMPLE
S1	Blocker (also known as a showstopper)	An issue that completely blocks the development process or testing of the game	Crashes or hangs as soon as you load into the game's front end; the next level does not load after completing the previous one
S2	Critical	An issue that hinders gameplay experience or development process	Game crashes, memory leaks, major FPS drops, objectives not completing
S3	High	Major loss of function that can impact the gameplay experience	Unable to reload a weapon after using reload button a few times
S4	Moderate	Moderate loss of function	Noticeable graphical issues flickering textures
S5	Trivial	Minor loss of function	Spelling mistakes on signs

an extensive list of components, so try your best to find the ones appropriate for your bug. Never submit a report without the components section filled in. Game modes could also be a component as many video games have different modes, such as single-player and different multiplayer modes, so having component labels can help filter those modes.

9.4 AFFECT VERSIONS

This is used to list the version of the game which is affected by the bug. There can be various versions of the game; some will be versions used for release, while others can be unreleased versions used internally by other departments. For example, the code team may make a separate development branch of the game to test experimental code or rework code to be integrated into the main development branch. QA may be requested to test a version of the game built from this separate branch, as there can be unique bugs not seen in the standard version of the game. Having a list of different version types will help developers and producers filter bugs that only impact specific build types.

9.5 BUILD IDS

This is where you will add information about the game version you found the bug on. A build ID can be made up of prefixes, suffixes, and change list numbers, which help provide the development teams with all the information about the exact version of the game on which the issue was found. Each company will have their own formatting when it comes to inputting build IDs, so make sure to stick to the approved format. Always double-check your IDs and even have a template of the format handy as a reminder.

9.6 STEPS TO REPRODUCE

So, you have found a bug, and you know how to reproduce it successfully, which is great. Now you need to explain to others how to do the same. Your reproduction steps (or repro steps) should have instructions on how to do this, starting from launching the game and ending with an observation step which briefly describes what the issue looks like. Try to keep the number of steps as short as possible.

When writing your repro steps you need to make sure they are clear and detailed enough for anyone to recreate the issue. Don't assume the person reading the report has prior knowledge of the game. There will be many members of the development team that won't have the hours of experience you have as a tester. So, adding keyboard keys or controller buttons to press for specific actions can be helpful. If there are CVARs or other debugs that can be used to speed up the steps, they can also be included in your report; however, you must explain in your description that you were able to reproduce the issue naturally.

9.7 DESCRIPTION

This section of the report will have the most details as it should contain any relevant information to help advise developers on the scale of the issue. For example, if you have tested other locations, you can inform them that the bug only occurs in a particular area of the game or multiple areas. This will let them know that the issue is game-wide or not. Another example can be items, weapons, and characters, as these can have variations for you to test. If you have tested them and found problems with some variations but not others, you could create a table listing all affected assets in the description section.

9.8 WORKAROUND

If you have encountered a severe issue that hinders your ability to test, sometimes there can be ways around the problem. You can do this in-game, or a CVAR that could assist in getting around the bug. Writing down a workaround can help other testers or developers who may be blocked from doing their work. If there isn't a workaround, you are okay to leave it blank.

9.9 EXPECTED RESULTS AND ACTUAL RESULTS

Here you write what is supposed to happen when following the reproduction steps and what actually happens. Don't just put a generic statement like "game shouldn't crash" or "game should work properly" for expected results, as these are redundant. Instead, briefly describe what should happen next when playing the game. Some bug reports may or may not have the actual results section as it could be redundant due to the description section and summary providing the same information set. But it could help clearly label the results of following the reproduction steps and comparing them with the intended outcome.

9.10 ATTEMPTS, OCCURRENCES, AND PERCENTAGES

These will be three separate sections on a bug report, but for formatting sake, we will bundle them all together so you see how it looks in a real-world scenario. This data shows the reader how many times you attempted to reproduce the issue. When you find a bug, you must check how often the issue can occur. Some bugs may only happen once; others can happen every time, so you need to make sure you have investigated the bug thoroughly and have been able to successfully reproduce the bug (which is your occurrence section). As a rule of thumb, you want to get a least three occurrences of an issue before bugging it. Depending on the company, they will have different procedures for bugs that happen only once.

Below is an example of how these sections can look in a bug report:

- *Attempts*: 5 (how many times you attempted to reproduce the bug)
- *Occurrences*: 3 (how many times the bug happened)
- *Percentages*: 60% (the issue occurs 60% of the time based on the number of occurrences and attempts)

9.11 AFFECT PLAYERS

What are the chances of the players seeing this issue? In your bug report, there could be a drop-down menu where you choose the different levels of likelihood players will encounter the problem (e.g. always, sometimes, rarely). This can be useful to developers and producers in prioritising matters when it comes time to bug-fixing periods.

9.12 ASSIGNEE

This is the person who is given the bug report. They will be responsible for looking over the issue to fix it or pass it to the appropriate developer.

QA testers at any level don't assign bugs directly to developers; this is the producers' job. Different companies will have their own guidelines for how QA should assign bugs. For example, in some companies, you must assign the bugs to the QA leads, who will then assign it to the appropriate producers.

Other companies may have a generic QA account that will act as a Jira bucket. QA leadership (usually seniors or leads) will review the issue to ensure that it has all the requirements before assigning it to a producer. Some companies may allow QA testers to assign bugs directly to producers after passing their probation.

If you are in a company that does this, always refer to documentation such as a team's grid or a producer assignment page. Don't forget there are multiple departments in a games studio; each department will have its own producer.

If there is an art issue, it must be assigned to a producer who overlooks the art department. Design, VFX, audio, animation, and more will have a producer assigned to that department. If you assign an issue to the wrong producer, it will delay the bug-fixing pipeline. Production doesn't assign bugs immediately after they are created, so if a bug is on the wrong person, it could take days or even weeks before the error is noticed and then assigned to the correct producer.

9.13 TEAM

This is essentially the department which the bug would be associated with. This helps to organise issues so they go to the correct people who can fix them. Like with the Assignee section, you are not responsible for assigning it to specific teams. That is the job of the producer. However, depending on the company, when you have created an issue, you may be required to assign it to the QA or production teams. If it's on the QA team, leadership will vet the bug and assign it to the production team. The production team will review the issue and assign it to the appropriate development teams and developers.

9.14 ATTACHMENTS

This is where you attach any relevant files to the bug report. The main limitation you will have is memory, your company may have a limited memory size for report attachments. So if you have a 4k video that is 1-minute long, that can easily be of size 300-400 MB. Depending on your internet connection, it could take a couple of minutes to download or even have horrible buffering times if you want to play in the web browser. You might not even be allowed to upload such a large file. Sites such as Jira might limit you to 150 MB upload.

Regarding videos, you must find the right balance between quality and file size. In some of your videos, you may have debug information on the screen, so if you have a low-quality video, it won't be useful because developers might be unable to read the information on the screen. You can provide screenshots alongside videos to help get clear image quality for developers to read debug information. Other files you may be required to upload could be any player or editor logs generated when playing the game or using the game engine.

Suppose you have a location-based issue that you are providing evidence for. It's important to show the issue and where and how to find it. For instance, if a particular area or corner of a room has a graphical issue, it's not very helpful to have a video just showing that one corner without any landmarks or references to the larger space. This can be frustrating for developers trying to fix the issue and the QA tester, who may have to retest the issue afterwards. Having videos that clearly show how to get to the locations is very helpful and can save a lot of time.

Types of Testing

10

10.1 BLACK BOX AND WHITE BOX TESTING

Black box testing is when a tester essentially plays the game like how the players will experience it. If you search the term black box, you will find the common metaphor that best describes this testing type. So, imagine that you put something into a black box (input), and then something comes out (output), but because the box is black, the user can't see the process happening within the box. With that in mind, the testers may be unable to see under the hood of a game, such as the game code. Most testing is done using black box testing as game testers don't need to know the inner workings of the game; instead, the testing focuses on the output, which is the outcome of the player's actions in the game.

Whereas white box is when testers can see the game's inner workings. Using the box metaphor again, rather than having a black box this time, the box is transparent, so you can see inside it when you put something into the box. You see the inner workings of how it outputs something to the other side.

There is also a third type of testing known as grey box testing. This isn't to be confused with greyboxing, where developers create a block out of a location to get a sense of the layout and gameplay. Grey box testing, in this scenario, is a software testing technique combining both black box and white box testing. This is when a tester will have some partial knowledge of coding and will have access to additional commands that allow testers to get access to debug information.

DOI: 10.1201/9781003314806-10

10.2 PLAYTEST

We've already discussed playtesting earlier in this book, but playtesting isn't just used on the public to get their feedback; it can also be done internally.

Due to the secrecy of video game development, the studio may not want to do large usability or public betas to get feedback. This is where QA comes in. When a new level, location, or new multiplayer mode has been developed, the QA department can be used for playtesting. QA will play the game similar to the end user; they will go through the critical paths of the main mission or complete multiplayer objectives. They will check if everything works as intended, noting any issues along the way. Still, the primary goal is to experience the game and provide qualitative feedback to developers on what does and doesn't work well. This feedback can assist in re-balancing gameplay and help make quality-of-life improvements.

10.3 PERFORMANCE TESTING

This test focuses on how well the game performs regarding its stability and responsiveness. The most notable performance issues you may encounter are frames-per-second (FPS) issues, such as FPS stuttering, being below benchmark, and long load times. For multiplayer games, network and server performance are issues that could occur when testing and can also be the basis for some of your dedicated performance testing.

Regarding FPS, different companies will have their rulings on what is acceptable and what targeted frame rates are. FPS can vary from hardware to hardware. For instance, you may be able to achieve a consistent 60 FPS on a PS5, but the same game on, say, the Nintendo Switch might only be able to achieve 30 due to its limited hardware in comparison to the PS5.

Some of the data that can be useful for developers are videos with any FPS information on screen to showcase where the large drops or stutters in performance occur. But also any CVARs and debug options that provide on-screen data about CPU and GPU utilisation. Being able to monitor how the hardware utilises its resources with the game can allow developers to optimise their work to reduce any high CPU or GPU usage from scaling game functionality, code refactoring to optimising visuals which use GPU such as VFXs, volumetrics (such as lighting, fog, water, clouds) to 3D geometry such as reducing polycount, adding levels of detail as ways to help optimise 3D assets.

When bugging performance issues, try to mitigate any possibility of false positives. For example, if you are testing on a PC, some browsers can take a nice chunk of your CPU, *Cough* Chrome *cough*. Background processes can slightly affect performance, but if you have any graphical intensive applications open like a game engine or two copies of same game running, this will also cause game performance to drop, creating a false positive.

10.4 LOAD TESTING

Load tests are a type of performance testing in which developers can analyse the performance of a system when it's under a lot of load. For games, this usually means when a player is trying to connect to a multiplayer server via login services. Manual testing would require a large team of testers to all log into a server to apply load to the backend services. However, this will pale in comparison with when the game goes live and you have players from all corners of the globe loading into the server. The QA department may have tools to simulate a more real-world scenario, for instance, headless clients, which are AI clients that will automatically load into the game to help simulate many people trying to load into the game simultaneously.

10.5 SOAK TESTING

Soak testing is the process of having the game run for a prolonged amount of time. This could be leaving the game idle, pausing the game, or staying idle at the title screen. Soak testing can be seen as a subset of both load and performance testing. The aim is to check how the software functions after 2, 5, or 10 hours of use. Is it still working as intended, or will it behave differently, such as slowdowns or crashes? As you can tell, it's a very time-consuming process. As such, manually testing this may be out of the question. Who has the hours to spend looking at a screening and waiting for something to happen? However, this process may have some level of automation to provide data on memory usage, logs of frame rate, and other performance metrics. This type of test can be beneficial to find defects within the software that developers might not be aware of, such as memory leaks, memory corruption, or even a gradual degradation of performance or response of software functions.

10.6 STRESS TESTING

Stress testing helps to verify the stability of a game under intense situations to see how well the game handles data when its infrastructure is pushed to it's limits. This type of testing is primarily used for multiplayer games, as developers will need to test if the servers and backend systems can handle different scenarios that could lead to connection errors or server crashes. It involves tests such as a large number of players loading into the game and playing it simultaneously as a way to push the servers to see if it can maintain its stability.

A lot of games during their launch period can experience some technical issues. An example that springs to my mind is the launch of GTA Online back in October 2013 on 7th generation platforms. Rockstar's flagship franchise is one of the most recognisable series in gaming history. Everyone wants to play it, and when GTA 5 online multiplayer was released, many people tried to play online. Sadly, many players could not access the online mode due to various server issues, games failing to load and disconnection issues.

Cynical gamers may think the company didn't thoroughly test their server. This couldn't be further from the truth, as these servers would have been tested internally, mainly using QA departments and possibly using automated testing such as headless clients to try and simulate what live servers will be like and push them as much as possible. Of course, you can test your systems as much as you want to prepare, but until a game is released to a broader audience, you never really know what will happen. Rockstar did comment about their server issue back in 2013:

> *One thing we are already aware of and are trying to alleviate as fast as we can, is the unanticipated additional pressure on the servers due to a significantly higher number of players than we were anticipating at this point.*
>
> *Quote from www.theguardian.com/technology/2013/oct/01/*
> *grand-theft-auto-online-launch*

Game journalist Austin Wood[1] did a great feature on GamesRadar back in February 2019 about online games, titled "It's Just Impossible". Devs explain why big online games always seem to break at launch". Gamers may think that multiplayer issues are due to problems with server capacity, but this isn't as much of an issue for developers as you may think. Developers will invest a lot in hardware to ensure they are ready to launch the game so that problems can stem from issues with online services and game software, such as a memory leak.

Another test could be pushing a games' features or mechanisms to the edge. Take, for example, fallout 76 with its infamous nuke server crashes. Users found that if you launched three nukes simultaneously, the resulting impact caused a server crash. Because players pushed this nuke feature, they were able to expose a fault with the game. As much as you can stress test online multiplayer internally, it will never beat the live player experience. Having players play the game is the best way for online games to get stress tested and ensure stability. Many multiplayer games use public betas because as much as you can do internal testing to ensure stability until it's out in the wild, you won't know how the game will hold up. And it can help expose many stability, performance, and general multiplayer issues that QA can report and for developers to prioritise fixes ready for the official launch.

10.7 COMPATIBILITY TESTING

This type of testing checks if your game will function on its hardware requirements for devices such as PC and mobile. With mobile, for instance, you need to consider if your game will run correctly on different android devices, as the market has a large collection of android devices with different screen sizes and processing abilities. Therefore, you may need to create tests to ensure the game runs and is stable on other devices and that the game's interface supports different screens. PC are similar as well. Because PCs are entirely customisable, you must ensure that different hardware configurations do not cause any issues for the player; for example, the game runs correctly on both AMD and Nvidia graphic cards.

Compatibility testing can also be done for home consoles to ensure that software can be uninstalled/installed without issues. As you know, many home consoles are not customisable. Your PS5 has the same hardware as someone else on your street. However, more and more games on consoles have options to optimise the game for performance and quality. Some also provide FPS boosts, so these may be something to consider for compatibility testing.

Control schemes can also fall under compatibility testing. If you have ever played a flight or racing sim on PC, you will be aware that there are many controllers on the market to help make you feel like you're in the driver's seat or cockpit. Those controllers will need testing with your game software to make sure they are working and compatible. The same goes for controllers for consoles as well. The Switch, for instance, has multiple ways to play one game with different controllers (pro-controller or Joy-Con). Some companies may also have controller smoke tests to ensure these devices still function as intended.

10.8 SMOKE TESTING

This type of test can be best described as a health check to ensure the stability of the game build. These tests are done to inform the wider QA team that a build is good enough to be used for more extensive testing. Smoke tests usually have broad coverage that quickly goes over major functionality to highlight any blocker or critical stability issues that would prevent further testing. Smokes should not take too long as they are intended to be done quickly due to their brief and broad nature. If you are manually doing smoke tests, they should be completed within a short time frame, approximately an hour maximum; if it's any longer, the test is far too complex and detailed. You don't want other testers or developers waiting too long for results. Because these tests are repeated frequently, developers can set up automated tests and tools to check stability (usually set up daily) and even produce reports for teams to review to make informed decisions about going with a build.

10.9 SANITY TESTING

Sanity testing or sanity checks (which they can also be referred to) are tests performed on a build with a few changes implemented, such as small code changes or bug fixes. This type of testing is also considered a subset of regression testing (more on that later in this chapter). These small changes to the build should be minor and pose little risk of bringing up new issues or threatening a build's stability. Sanity tests are done on relatively stable build that has passed its smoke test. The tester will focus on specific areas or components with those changes or fixes. Because of this, sanity testing is much narrower than smoke tests as you focus on a few areas or functions to ensure they are working as intended.

10.10 RETESTING

This might not be the most fun task, but it's very important. Retesting is where you will reproduce bugs that developers have resolved and confirm if they are indeed fixed. If the bug is confirmed fixed by QA, you can safely close the report as "done" and comment that the issue no longer occurs. However, if the issue still happens, you must re-open it and assign it to the appropriate department. Sometimes you will have to assign it to the lead QA who will then hand the bug over to producers or, depending on the company you work for, allow you to assign it to the correct producer.

When retesting, one vital thing to note is to compare the fix change number and the date the issues were resolved on the report, to the build you are working on. A quick simple example would be if a bug has been fixed and integrated into build that has change number 20 and you are using the build with change number 18, you won't be able to verify the fix until you have downloaded a build with same change number or higher that has the supposed fix present.

Retesting isn't just done on resolved issues but can also be done on issues that are open, reopened, or in a department's backlog. As the game you are testing is in active development, people will constantly update and change it. Sometimes, they may fix issues along the way, or other people's changes can resolve existing issues. Because of this, some bugs can become redundant. Retesting opened or backlog issues can be a part of tasks for the day or can be requested by others, such as producers. If an issue is still present, you must update the report with build ID that you used to retest the issue (you may also need to add the affects version if necessary). Attaching new logs and screenshots to the report is also recommended. Maybe the bug you are retesting has evolved slightly and isn't exactly same as the one initially reported. In that case, you can amend the summary, add new reproduction steps, and make a comment to inform others of the changes made. If you are unsure what to do in this situation, it's always best to consult seniors or leads. They can advise you to either change the issue or close it off and make a whole new report, as sometimes it's best to have a clean slate to avoid any confusion about the current issue.

10.11 REGRESSION

The terms retesting and regression can be somewhat interchangeable in game testing. In fact, when I started in QA, regression was the primary term used to describe checking resolved issues to confirm if they were fixed. However, it was only recently that I learnt the clear distinction between retesting and regression so that it is consistent with the software testing terminology.

Regression is the process of testing existing sections and functions of a game to ensure they have not degraded in quality. So why is this type of testing done? For example, say you and your team have done extensive testing and retesting on a particular level for a while. You left the level knowing it is relatively bug-free, only to return a month later to find everything is on fire. So, what happened? It can be due to updates or changes in the game code because development teams will be fixing bugs and regularly adding new features and functions to the game, which can affect existing content. This means that the tester needs to go back and sweep areas for any issues, as changes to code can create new bugs or exploits. Regression testing becomes a more frequent task with large multiplayer-focused games such as live service games like massively multiplayer online games (MMOs). Because new content will be added, there could also be code changes or even refactoring old code to make it more efficient. These changes could cause new issues to occur. So, QA will need to regress features or area that uses these new changes to ensure the quality and stability for the players. That isn't to say single players don't require regression as, again, new architectures and upgrades to a game engine or gameplay mechanics can occur during development, which will mean regression is an inevitable part of testing.

10.12 AD-HOC TESTING (FREE TESTING)

Ad-hoc testing, also known as free testing, is where you can freely explore the game and test it however you want. Due to the unique nature of video games in the entertainment media, players can interact in a game world in various ways. The whole purpose of ad-hoc testing is for you to explore and attempt to break and even exploit the game's mechanics, features, and even the game world itself. There are hundreds if not thousands of possible variations on how you can approach a mission or an environment, and it would be almost impossible for someone to create a comprehensive checklist for every single possible variable, so ad-hoc testing will allow you to bring out your creative side of testing so try to think out of the box. Players can do almost anything they want in a video game, so it's up to you to try out as many variables as possible to see what causes issues and effectively report these.

10.13 COMPONENT TESTING

Component testing in software testing terms is when testing is done on individual components. In terms of game development, it's similar. You may be required to focus on testing specific gameplay features or mechanics. Maybe, you need to test a new combat system, so you will have test cases and an area that concentrates solely on this aspect of the game. A great example of this is the Spider-Man 4 Wii developer build leak (you can search for videos on YouTube that show the various test levels the game has). One of the levels is a test area for testing out Spider-Man's traversal mechanics, such as wall jumping, running, and various web-swinging abilities.

10.14 TESTING ENVIRONMENTS

So, you may be wondering where you will spend most of your time testing. Well, this might be a no-brainer, but most testers will find themselves working in the actual game itself, loading into the game from a PC or console. Although this is where you will spend most of your time, others in specialist roles like embedded may find themselves in slightly different testing environments. Some testers work within the game engine itself; as Chapter 1 discusses, technical QA roles may require testers to focus their efforts on the game engine to test its stability or any in-house tools.

Many new features or gameplay mechanics need a separate location to test in to ensure they function as intended before being integrated into the wider game. These are known as test levels; these can be set up in the game engine or made playable in a build. These rooms will have little to no final art (or at the very least, placeholder art) and can be made up of just blocks. Again, this ties in with component testing as these areas allow developers to isolate the features that require testing .

Sometimes a different game version may be created for specific development teams to focus on and implement their work. This is a type of version control known as branching (another term that can be used is feature streams). If a new feature or system is being reworked, having a separate branch allows teams to work in parallel. It separates any "work in progress" features and code from the main branch to ensure overall stability. Before a feature from the feature branch is merged back into the main one, QA will test this different version of the game to review the new features and see how it works with the existing game, as new features will create new issues and exploits. Once QA do their pass and the bugs have been resolved, then in theory, when the branched code/features are merged over, it shouldn't destabilise the main branch too much.

10.15 TEST CASES AND SUITES

During testing, you will be required to fill in test documentation to help track progress. This can be done using software such as TestRail, Excel, or other project management tools. So let's break down what you can expect from these test cases and suites.

10.15.1 Test Cases

These refer to individual tests that a tester must carry out to verify that a particular element or function of the game is working as intended. You can think of these as instructions on what you're testing and even how to test this function. Table 10.1 provides a basic example of what a test case can look like. Depending on who created the cases, they can be fairly straight forward or can have a bit more complexity to their setup. So, let's break down the different components of a possible test case.

10.15.1.1 Test Case ID

Many test cases will be created during the development of a game (easily be in the hundreds if not thousands depending on the game's complexity). Having clear identifiers for test cases can make highlighting any cases with severe defects to leadership easier. Many test cases will also be very similar and could be reused for different sections of the game. For instance, a general art check for level 1 can easily be copied and repurposed for level 2. Having a clear ID can help distinguish between two cases that are essentially the same, just used

TABLE 10.1   Basic example of test cases

TEST NUMBER	TITLE	DESCRIPTION	TESTER	STATUS
01	Options menu: Sound slider	The player should be able to increase and decrease SFX, music, and dialogue using the sound slider in the options menu and hear the changes in game	JDoe	Passed
02	Options menu: Subtitles	Players can toggle subtitles on/off	JDoe	Failed

elsewhere. You may have to manually create ID numbers, use formulas (e.g. for Excel) that allow you to make them quickly, or if you use test case software such as TestRail, it will automatically generate a unique ID for each test case you create.

10.15.1.2 Title

This is the name of the test. The name can be based on your testing component, for example, collision, VFX. Like a bug report summary, it should be descriptive so a tester knows what the test is and pass the criteria by reading the title.

10.15.1.3 Description

This has a function similar to the tile; this section can give further information on what the test case covers. Depending on your test case formatting, this section may not be required as the title can provide enough context for the tester.

10.15.1.4 Pre-conditions

These are any additional steps a tester must do before running this test case. For example, specific setup or requirements may be needed for a particular test. Other examples could be requiring multiplayer elements (matchmaking, needing multiple players), a specific feature or system, or getting to certain sections of a game.

10.15.1.5 Steps

Test cases can have steps attached to them (TestRail, e.g., has a section where one can add steps). These detail what the user must do to reach the scenario that is outlined in the title and description. These steps should be easy to understand and follow. Like a bug report, don't write these steps assuming the user has the same amount of knowledge of the game as you have. Try to make it as accessible as possible.

10.15.1.6 Expected Results

It's essential to pay attention to this section as it describes the intended behaviour for the feature that you are testing. So even if you aren't 100% familiar with some regions of a game or its systems, the expected results will help you understand what is supposed to happen.

10.15.1.7 Status

This section is to show the recent results of the test, whether it was successful, and met the expected results or failed due to a bug. Status can have a drop list of status options for you to choose from, such as pass, fail, pass with issues (test can be completed but will encounter a bug during it), blocked (an issue from a previous test prevents you from completing following test), N/A (not applicable), retest (if the issue that blocked or failed a test has been resolved can set the status to retest so it can be rechecked).

10.15.1.8 Tester

This will be the name of the person who completed the test. This is useful to ensure people don't accidentally repeat a test and give accountability and responsibility to the tester.

10.15.1.9 Bug Link

Here you would provide a link to any relevant bug reports related to the test case you are working on. This is a must on test cases that have issues, failed, or blocked. It is helpful to link all these issues as they can be presented to leadership to show the status of a feature and the related issues so they can action them.

10.15.1.10 Notes

Notes are any additional comments worth mentioning for other members of the team.

10.15.1.11 Time

This is where you log how long it took to complete a test case. Not all test suites will have this, but some can; for example, TestRail will have a start/stop button for each test case to track time. This can be helpful for QA leadership to see how long a test suite is taking to complete and give estimated completion times to production based on the time taken so far with test cases.

You can see some similarities between the components of a test case to a bug report. Not every aspect listed earlier will be in a test case. Depending on the type of test you are doing, and even the software, some of these can be omitted. When I have done test cases on an Excel sheet for certain game functions or locations, sections like steps or pre-conditions may not be necessary as the title and description should provide enough context for the tester to complete the case.

10.15.2 Test Suite

These are a collection of test cases, a good metaphor I have read in the past is to imagine a test suite like a bookcase in a library. Those books aren't just placed randomly on a shelf. They are organised in a way that is easily accessible to anyone, for example, by genre (romance, horror, etc.). Test suites allow you to group test cases and categorise them for what you plan to test. Say you are testing characters with unique abilities in a multiplayer shooter. If you were to create a test suite for that character, you might have a collection of test cases relating to them, such as animations, passive effects, abilities, art, and SFX. You need to try and think of every aspect of that character and their mechanics to make sure they have been thoroughly covered during your testing.

Test suites and cases are constantly evolving documents. As a game is still in active development, levels can be altered or cut, and new features and mechanics will be introduced. As such, QA needs to be aware of these changes so the appropriate alternations and additions can be made in their test cases and suite to ensure the testers have the most updated and correct information on tests. Dan Gronner explains well why it's important to keep tests up to date.

> *Even if you have a great test case that perfectly covers a mechanic or an area of the game, in two months' time, if no one, taking responsibility for that, it's very likely to be out of date. And at worst, that means you can become blinded to risks that emerge as things change.*
>
> *Quote from Dan Gronner*

NOTE

1   Austin Wood. "It's Just Impossible": Devs explain why big online games always seem to break at launch. Available at: https://www.gamesradar.com/its-just-impossible-devs-explain-why-big-online-games-always-seem-to-break-at-launch/. Published on February 22, 2019.

Looking after Yourself (Mental Health and Your Rights)

11

11.1 MENTAL HEALTH IN THE GAMES INDUSTRY

It's important to look out for your well-being. Mental health awareness over the last decade (hell, maybe even a bit more than that) has been on the increase due to many factors, from the hard work of advocacy groups (charities like Mind), influencers, celebrities, or anybody openly sharing their stories which help people understand and challenge status quo and change stigmas surrounding mental health. I spoke with Sky Tunley-Stainton and Rosie Taylor, who work for Safe in Our World, a mental health organisation explicitly aimed at the games industry. They have discussed their insights on mental health and its impact on the industry.

> *there is stigma around mental health, but I think there's more stigma around mental illness, and there's the distinction between the two. Sometimes, when people refer to the term mental health, people automatically think something negative and sad, and maybe someone who's depressed. That is a part of mental health but mental health can also be positive. It's not just about negativity.*
>
> *Everyone has mental health, everyone has health, and I think it should be considered as dual purpose. Everyone talks about how they have a cold and is crying about it because it's miserable. But no one will*

talk about the fact that maybe they're feeling really anxious. And in my head, the two should be the same, but they're not because you still get funny looks if you say "oh, I had a panic attack the other day".

People are like, "oh my God, why are you bringing that to work? That's so weird". And it's not; it's just how it should be. But then, on the flip side of that, we're still seeing poor representation of people, with mental health conditions in media, in TV, film and games.

And it all adds to the stigma because if you're not educating people appropriately about these conditions and what is associated with them, it can be very damaging to the stigmatisation around that specific mental health illness. It's a challenging one, and I think it is getting there, and we are seeing people who want to be able to represent people better and more accurately.

Quote from Rosie Taylor

So why am I discussing this in a book about getting into the game industry? Well, it's to help give some insights into some of the less than pleasant experiences faced by people within the industry, like burnout, crunch, and overtime. The game industry is driven by a hardworking and passionate workforce which can sadly be exploited. Many people want to work in the video game industry and want to prove themselves. Because of this, many will find themselves putting in a lot more work hours due to the pressures of tight deadlines and mandates from higher-ups or even a sense of responsibility and loyalty to the game they're working on.

it's important to highlight mental health in any industry, and it's not something that is specific to the games industry. However, the games industry has grown incredibly quickly. And it's also potentially an industry that's more at risk for issues surrounding mental health, because of a lot of crunch culture. Because of a lot of high expectations that are put on people within that industry.

Quote from Sky Tunley-Stainton

We need to look after people who are passionate about it, but also set those boundaries and make sure that they're not, working double time for something that they really don't need to and don't burn out.

Quote from Rosie Taylor

When people think of games, they usually think of the company behind it. They never really think about the human faces behind them. When you compare games to the film industry, more people can name drop or recognise prominent directors, actors, and screenwriters. In contrast, if you were to ask someone about a major producer, writer, or designer for a video game, you'd probably only be able to name a handful (if that). People don't necessarily think about the human faces behind video game development. They're more familiar with just the faceless company, franchises or the company logo. As a result, it's easy to forget the hundreds, if not thousands, of people that have worked for years to make a game a reality.

If you are reading this book, you are interested in being a part of the industry and should be aware of what people have to deal with. You can't feign ignorance about some of the hardships your possible peers are dealing with. A particular sub-group of "gamers" will brush off overtime and crunch as a necessary evil. Sadly, even some people in the industry see it as a necessity or something to factor in during project management.

Try to pace yourself. It's easy to go over the top or to do excessive hours. Overtime and crunch are big issues in the game industry, leading to many people burning out and leaving it altogether. Always take care of yourself first, if you feel stressed or have too much workload. Remember that you're working on a game, you're not saving lives. A former colleague and dear friend has said this to me many times. But, of course, playing videos can be a great way of relieving stress, a form of escapism and has helped people during difficult times. But those experiences shouldn't come at the expense of the physical and mental well-being of the developers.

Overtime is when you are asked to do additional hours on top of your contractual work hours. In general, this is requested when a deadline is approaching. Most of the time, any additional hours you are doing are paid; however, there have been instances in the past where people have done a lot of extra hours without being fairly compensated. Some companies may offer toil instead of the extra pay as an alternative. Overtime policies will change from company to company. Some will have it as an option, others may make it mandatory. I have seen instances where overtime is optional, but if they don't get the required hours needed, they will make it compulsory for those not providing enough extra hours. Overtime isn't just for additional hours during the work week but can also bleed into the weekend, so you may be asked to do half a day or a few hours on a Saturday or Sunday, depending on the project's needs.

It can be easy to be intimidated or somewhat pressured into providing extra hours as if everyone else is chipping in more time and you're not. You may wonder if people, especially management, will look down on you for doing that. Have a look at what the legal limit is in your country. Take the UK as an example, the legal limit is 48 hours. It may be worth having a conversation about overtime with the manager if you have responsibilities outside of work that prevent you from doing overtime or a certain amount. If you are getting overworked, some extreme measures could be putting in an official complaint through HR, going to a union or leaving, and getting work at a place with an anti-crunch policy (many game companies advertise this on their job pages).

11.2 BURNOUT

Burnout is included in the World Health Organization's (WHO) International Classification of Diseases (ICD-11), it is not classified as a medical condition but is known as an occupational phenomenon. So, first thing you should do is recognise the signs of burnout and see if it's affecting you.

> *Burn-out is a syndrome conceptualized as resulting from chronic work-place stress that has not been successfully managed. It is characterized by three dimensions*:
>
> * *feelings of energy depletion or exhaustion;*
> * *increased mental distance from one's job, or feelings of negativism or cynicism related to one's job;*
> * *reduced professional efficacy.*
>
> *Quote from www.who.int/news/item/28-05-2019- burn-out-an-occupational-phenomenon-international-classification-of-diseases*

Burnout has led to many people leaving the industry. The average length of someone in the industry can be from 3 to 5 years, and that's mainly because of the stresses of the job, which causes people to burn out and leave.

Some ways to reduce the effects of burnout include setting boundaries for yourself and management, knowing when it's appropriate to work and setting those limits. With managers, make sure they don't message you at inappropriate times, such as weekends or out of hours. If your manager gives you a lot of work, maybe discuss spreading work more evenly to reduce your stress and workload. Set time aside for breaks, holidays, and activities with friends or yourself. Take time away from work to focus on living your life to give your mind and body the break it needs. Maybe even disconnect from your phone and social media, as you will be tempted to check work email and may end up doom scrolling.

If you feel that your mental health is declining, try to find help, don't bottle things away or avoid dealing with your issues, as it can be very unhealthy. I should know as I did this myself in my previous job as a teacher. Many elements of my personal and professional life were going sideways. Everything I worked hard to build since leaving university seemed to be falling apart. I thought I could ignore it, be tough, man up, and other similar phrases I had heard throughout my life until that point. Instead, it turned me into a sad, bitter, angry, and spiteful human. I felt broken and decided that I needed to make a change. I spoke to my manager, who was able to help me get counselling and reasonable adjustments to my work. These helped me start to unpack some of the issues I was having, slowly open up more, and heal a little. As the saying goes, "It's okay to not be okay". You don't have to hide how you are doing. If you have supportive friends, family, and co-workers, it can help to talk to them.

If you trust your line manager and they support their team members, then it's worth having a conversation with them if you are struggling with mental health issues. Perhaps the HR department (human resources) can help if you can't approach them. Companies can provide some mental health support, such as referrals to services like counselling . It may be worth learning if any mental health first-aiders are in your company. Some companies may offer 1 or 2 duvet days per year. If you haven't heard of this before, this is when an employee can take time off without advance notice. We all have had those days when we didn't want to work, to rest up. This isn't due to any perceived laziness but could be due to stress from work and temporary burnout caused by a particularly busy period.

11.3 IMPOSTER SYNDROME

Have you ever had a job or were doing your academics and had your head filled with self-doubt, feelings of inadequacy, or you think to yourself, "Why am I here? I don't deserve to be here" (e.g. shouldn't be in a particular job). You may have been hit with imposter syndrome, which can best be described as a persistent inability to see your own success and will continue to doubt your skills, and accomplishments, and internalised fear of being exposed as a fraud.

Imposter syndrome can affect you in different ways because you feel you need to prove you belong. This could lead to some unhealthy work practices. You may overwork yourself or even self-sabotage, such as holding yourself back from seeking career opportunities, being less willing to speak up about suggestions, or discussing issues and concerns.

> *People who enter this industry do it because they are so passionate about it, and they've had a lifelong love of gaming. And when they enter the industry, they almost can't believe it. And they think, what have I done to fool these people into thinking I'm capable? When are they gonna find out that I'm a fraud?*
>
> *It can lead to a lot of things. It can lead to someone experiencing anxiety. It can lead to someone overworking themselves to the point of burnout because they're trying so desperately to live up to this expectation that they think other people have of them. Feeling like you haven't earned your place.*
>
> *It's not something that is specific to the games industry, but it is something that is a lot worse in this type of industry because of the high regard in which it's held. And it being someone's dream job and when they get it, they maybe don't feel like they deserve it.*
>
> *Quote from Sky Tunley-Stainton*

If you start feeling like an imposter, you might think you are the only one, but that isn't true. Many people in the industry have had to deal with the effects of imposter syndrome. Regardless of their success and status, everyone has doubted themselves at some point. You can try and mitigate the effect of imposter syndrome in a few ways.

Try creating a list of successes and achievements, write down any accomplishments and save any comments or emails from others, like your line manager who praised your work. You can look back at these whenever you start to question your ability. Make sure you own these accomplishments. Don't downplay them by saying it's "just luck", be proud of your role in your successes and celebrate them. Tell yourself that you have done awesome work and are proud of it. Finally, try to let go of perfectionism. Trying to be "perfect" at your task or job doesn't help you; it's counterproductive and only feeds into your imposter syndrome. Understand that it's okay not to be perfect because trying to reach this perfect outcome can be unrealistic. Even if there are mistakes and some failures, reframe them into learning opportunities.

11.4 GAMING-SPECIFIC MENTAL HEALTH ORGANISATIONS

Some organisations around mental health are specially aimed towards the game industry that you can follow and learn more about. Below you will learn about some of the prominent ones within the industry.

11.4.1 TIGS

TIGS stands for the International Games Summit. It's a game development summit with various talks around mental health issues that the industry faces. The talks are spread over 2 days with many prominent keynote speakers. These talks and workshops are also virtual through Zoom or Twitch. You can learn more by visiting their website: tigs.ca/.

11.4.2 Safe in Our World

Safe in Our World's mission is to create more mental health awareness within the video game industry. Their site provides resources to its readers, from helplines to articles about mental health and the game industry. In addition, they do a lot of great work to call on developers and publishers to provide their employees more support, resources, and training around mental health.

They also have a podcast hosted by Rosie Taylor (who was awesome enough to speak with me for this book). These podcasts focus on mental health in video games and the game industry. Many people invited onto the podcast are gaming community members, from voice actors to streamers and game developers. All of them share their stories about mental health, which is a great way to reduce the stigma surrounding this topic and humanise people behind the scenes and what they face regarding mental health.

They have also worked with Mind Fitness (which provides training and coaching on well-being and mental health) to provide training courses on various subjects around mental health that tie directly with the industry. Most training courses are paid, so if you are currently working in the industry, it could be worth advocating for the company to provide training for staff. More info about the organisation can be found at safeinourworld.org/.

11.4.3 Check Point

Check Point provides mental health resources for game developers and the wider gaming community, such as gamers and streamers. Like Safe in Our World, the organisation's site offers resources for the gaming community, such as helplines. There are also free PDF books around self-care for developers.

Check Point has done several public-speaking events for various international conventions, such as GDC. They have a dedicated page on their website which links videos of these talks, which can be used to learn more about mental health and the game industry. You can use the following link to learn more about them: checkpointorg.com/.

11.5 UNIONS AND WORKERS' RIGHTS

If you follow the game development scene, you would have heard prominent game developers, journalists, and articles discussing working conditions, the call for more unionisation, and better standards in the industry overall. There has been more and more vocal support for unionisation within the industry. The games workforce love their work, and they are hugely passionate about their craft, but they also want to see improvements in the workplace, they want to see toxic and harmful practices eradicated, and they want a better work-life balance. Sometimes those issues can't be fixed internally, so unionising would allow them to fight for their rights and have the necessary protections.

IWGB Game Workers and Game Workers Unite are two prominent ones in the UK and the USA, respectively. In fact, in the USA, some game companies have been attempting to form their own unions for better working conditions, despite attempts from companies trying to use union-busting techniques to try and demoralise and discourage game workers. Nevertheless, the voices for change are getting louder, and support for better conditions is only getting stronger.

I would advise you to understand your rights as a worker, what an employer legally must provide, what counts as unfair treatment and even unfair dismissal from work to fight back if needed. QA can get some harsh treatment when crunch periods start, so make sure you know if you are legally entitled to overtime and the maximum overtime you are allowed to do, as this may help avoid overworking yourself.

Just writing about this makes me slightly worried as I might get blackballed by some people for suggesting joining or starting your own union (though I do hope that is just my own anxiety talking). But I feel it's essential for you, the person reading this, to start building your knowledge and make your own decisions on this matter. Sadly, I wish I could add more to this section, but I am still learning a lot about unions and workers' rights myself and have been actively encouraging people in my own life to learn more about these subjects. So, hopefully, you might start your own journey in learning more about these topics.

Where to Go Next

12

With any job, you may hit your threshold when you feel that you've done everything you can within that role. You need a new challenge, especially within video games. If you're working on the same project for a long time, at some point creatively you may feel like you need to move on to a new project. Once you start to feel unfulfilled in your role, it would be the best time to start looking to move on to a different company or progress within that company into a different position. If you don't decide to move forward, you may find that your work may start to slip slightly as you're not feeling motivated or challenged to keep the high standards up. I've had to deal with a few times where I felt like my role was becoming a little samey, and I noticed that my quality of work was slipping. But once I was presented with a new challenge that helped reinvigorate my motivation.

We have already discussed moving upwards in QA, but at some point, you may want to venture out and try other roles in and out of the industry. This might be slightly strange for me to write about as I spent nearly a whole chapter very early in this book explaining that QA isn't just a launching pad into other departments. But I understand that everyone has their own career ambitions, which can change over time, or maybe you always intended for QA to be a temporary job to get to your desired role. In fact, according to Skillsearch QA data, 69% QAs would consider moving into a different discipline. Which is fair, and I want to try to advise anyone. So here are just a few alternative routes you could go down.

12.1 SOFTWARE TESTING

Games are software, so you may think that it is natural to transition from games testing into QA for the IT industry, and while yes this is possible, it can be a bit more complex. It is also worth noting that if you are serious about moving from games to software testing, many need certifications from originations such as International Software Testing Qualifications Board (ISTQB) in software testing to transition. Some may need this as a requirement, but others may see this as desirable.

12.2 PRODUCTION

I decided to put this as a separate section because QA works closely with producers, so moving from QA into the production pipeline is natural. Many highly profiled producers working within the game industry started in QA. Production and QA work closely daily. Producers constantly communicate with QA about new areas or features that need testing, providing them with updates on development. On the other hand, QA can provide production with a realistic picture of a project's current state. Because you are exposed to some of the QA/production pipelines and processes, it gives you that base knowledge to help you transition into a production role. The best way to prove you are capable of a producer role is to build some leadership skills, maybe take on some extra responsibility in QA, such as being a point of contact for a test suite or helping to organise playtests. It's worth learning about project methodologies such as agile and waterfall if production is where you want to go.

12.3 DEVELOPMENT

Some of you may wish to go into an active development role such as art, design, or even programming. If you are trying to transition, my best advice would be to transition internally, as there is a better chance that the company you are working for will take you on in a junior position as you are already working for them. Most companies will be happy to develop their internal staff. If you go for, say, a design role at an external company, this will be very tricky without a good portfolio, and you probably have better success if you were going for their QA roles.

The second piece of advice I would give is to learn the internal pipeline and tools of the department you are interested in joining. Many development phases are universal between different studios, such as white box and grey box. But each company will have their own unique processes, so learning and understanding them is crucial if you want to transition out of QA. The same goes for internal tools; the company would have spent time developing tool kits for the game engine, art tools, etc., to help speed up or make development easier for different teams. Learning these will be a plus, so start reading any internal documentation and videos to help you upskill yourself.

The main challenge you will face is time. You will need to dedicate time to learning the core fundamentals of the discipline you are trying to go down. For example, say you what to be an environment artist, then you need to know how to use 3D art software, create textures and materials, and understand art techniques like using trim sheets and modular assets. From the example above, if you lack these skills and cannot demonstrate you can hit the quality expected for the project, you won't get that art job. Try to find out if there is any dedicated self-development time at your company. Maybe they give you 1 day a month for this; perhaps they don't have this. If that's the case, then your time management will be more critical as you must find a balance between work, personal life, and your own self-development. If you need guidance on how to upskill yourself, Chapter 3 may have some valuable suggestions.

QA is very similar to production in the sense that, much like a producer or project manager, a QA lead will know a lot about what's going on in the project. They'll know every single area of the game. They'll know who's working on what. A QA Lead will also have to delegate tasks and manage deadlines. Your transition from QA to production is quite natural, and a lot of people that I know who are in production have come from QA.

Alternatively, your options aren't limited to just production. You can always go into different areas in the gaming industry, but it's a lot easier if you're migrating within your company. So, if you want to have a stint at biz dev for example, and you're good at communicating with people, at sales pitching, you can have a whack at it. If there is a position opening for any junior roles, you can apply for those too. It's easier to get an interview for an internal position however, if you're applying externally and don't have any background or experience, then you're going to find it very tough to get an interview.

Quote from Naveen Yadav

I've definitely seen it happen a few times. Usually, you have to prove that you are willing to put in the work to learn the role before you even get it. I've seen a couple of people who have moved from QA to design, who had to independently learn how to design games in their own time. And had to put together, essentially a portfolio so that they could apply for a position and have a chance against all of these university degree design students.

Because you are in with the company, and you already know people and they know that you're gonna get on with them, you do have some advantage in that way. It can definitely happen, but it's not massively common in some roles, like design. It's a lot more common into something that there's a lot more transferable skills, like production where it's a lot of organization and timekeeping.

Quote from Darren Eggerton

12.4 CLOSING REMARKS

Sadly our time together has now come to an end, and we were growing so close! But joking aside, I do hope that you have been able to gain some insights and knowledge into QA, the different jobs and skills needed, as well as some good advice that you can use for your possible job applications and maybe even some help for when you start your first day as a tester.

When I started writing this book, I didn't just want to advise on getting a job as a QA tester. Instead, I wanted to take this as an opportunity to discuss many elements of the games industry, from mentorship to mental health, why? Because I believe that you should be aware of topics actively discussed within the industry because they can affect you. Despite some of the older stereotypes of QA being viewed as outsiders, they are a part of the industry, and their voices need to be heard in these matters. My intention is to prepare you for the industry as a QA tester and give you the knowledge to make informed decisions about where you choose to work. With all that said, I will bid you farewell and wish you luck on your journey.

Printed in the United States
by Baker & Taylor Publisher Services